Relax your Body, Quiet your Mind

52 Ways to Relieve Stress and Go Within

By Michele Geyer

Photographs by Michele Geyer
Sacred Body Card Images & Cover Design by Melanie Pahlmann

Logo Design by Jean Lehman

Sacred Body Oracle & Cards™
The Energetic Connection, LLC
Olympia, WA

Copyright © 2021 by the Energetic Connection, LLC;
Sacred Body Cards™

Relax Your Body Quiet Your Mind
ISBN# 978-0-9912521-3-8

All rights reserved, including the right to reproduce this book or portions thereof in any form whatsoever. Scanning, printing, copying, in any way uploading and electronic sharing of any part of this book without the permission of the author is unlawful piracy and theft of the author's intellectual property.

Please See Terms of Use:
www.sacredbodypathworking.com/terms-of-use.html

Prior written permission must be obtained for any use of the material from the book.
www.sacredbodypathworking.com/contact.html

Printed in the United States of America

Dedications

This book is dedicated to the courageous souls who have lived with anxiety, panic, or even just the stress of our times.

And to my parents who taught me well about flow and the high road of embracing the virtuous energies of:

Gratitude
Kindness
Caring
Respect
Humility
Understanding
Acceptance
Grace
Trust
Love
Joy
Action

It is dedicated to all those
whose practices I've learned along the way.

Especially the natural laws of giving & receiving.

Table of Contents

Preface	1
Health and Exercise Considerations	9
Introduction	10
Using this Book	10
The Sacred Body Oracle & Cards	11
Practicing	12
Elements of Stress	21
Anatomy and Energy of Relaxation	25
Definitions	30
Weekly Relaxation Practices: *Gateways & Stepping Stones*	38
Organic Body	40
1-Respiration—Receptive Breath	42
2-Digestion—Belly Breath	44
3-Circulation—Pooling Breath	46
4-Restoration—Connected Breath	48
5-Communication—Your Energy Field	50
The Lower World	52
The Elements	54
6-Eastern Wind—Sounds of the Sea	56
7-Southern Sun—Golden Suns	58
8-Western Sea—Ocean Waves	60
9-Northern Cave—Grounding	62
10-As Above, So Below—The Center of Your Head	64
Sacred Cisterns	66
11-Physical Body—Earth Energy	68
12-Etheric Body—Subtle Body Breath	70
13-Astral Body—Heavenly Cocoon	72
14-Mental Body—Spinal Breath	74
15-Spiritual Body—Cosmic Energy	76
The Veils of the Three Worlds	78

Relax your Body, Quiet your Mind

Rivers & Streams	80
16-Vital Vessels—Humming Breath	82
17-Sources—The Lower Cauldron	84
18-Anchorage—Grounding Spaces	86
19-The Riverbed—Yin & Yang	88
20-Tributaries—Ebb & Flow	90
21-Streams—The Central Channel	92
22-Wellsprings—Gender Grounding	94
23-Pools of Energy—The Golden Coin	96
The Middle World	98
Soul to Soul	100
24-Connection—Imprinting	102
25-Origins—The Wave	104
26-Clear Sight—The Space Behind your Eyes	106
27-Expressions—Rainbow Breath	108
28-Envisioning—Creating a Better Picture	110
29-Consciousness—Ocean Fog, Inland Heat	112
30-Impressions—Transparent Body	114
31-Balance—Clearing the Inner Kingdom	116
32-Knowingness—Alchemizing Breath	118
33-Telepathy—Thought Bubbles	120
34-The Witness—The Big Dipper	122
35-The Record Keeper—The Polestar	124
36-Healing—Springs of Gold	126
Mystical Journey	128
37-Strength—Heart Breath	130
38-Compassion—Your Halo	132
39-Brilliance—Cosmic Essence	134
40-Evolution—Three Minds	136
41-Vitality—Know Thyself	138
42-Expansion—Rest Pose	140
43-Intelligence—Emotional Expression	142
44-Wisdom—The Chrysalis	144

Windows to the Soul	146
Breath of Life	148
Visualization	150
Running Energy	152
Inner Rhythms	154
Cultivating Creativity	156
Self-Inquiry & Reflection	158
Awakening Awareness	160
Self-Healing & Mastery	162
The Upper World	164
Gateways to the Heights	166
45-Body Currents—Inner Compass	168
46-Earth & Cosmic Energies—Definition	170
47-Vortexes—Your Vitality Port	172
48-Primordial Power—Cranial Sacral Breath	174
49-Life Forces—Scouring Breath	176
50-Divine Matrix—Your Torus	178
51-Creative Energy—Co-Creativity	180
52-Spiritual Essence—Inner Constellations	182
Unity	184
The End is the Beginning	184
References	186
Biographical	188

Preface

Breakthrough

It was 1983. I was 26 years old and thought I was having a heart attack. I couldn't breathe and my heart was jumping out of my chest as I floated above my body—still close enough to feel the fear and but not quite enough to connect to myself. I had one repeating thought: *I'm going to die.*

This first panic attack came during the movie "Gandhi," in one of the largest theaters in the Bay Area. I was in the middle of the row, right in the middle of the theatre. Because I felt trapped and couldn't get out until intermission, the experience built and built.

I had never felt feel supported in life, and I couldn't bring myself to tell the two people next to me what was happening. So, I hovered over a toilet in the theatre restroom for the whole second half of the movie. When my friends asked me later in the lobby where I'd been, I told them I was sick and described a few of my symptoms. The older of the two said, "sounds like toxic shock. Are you using a tampon?"

Well, it wasn't that. And I didn't really find out what it was for many months, after a long slew of pretty much daily panic attacks during the summer of 1983.

Although I fought with these same experiences for five years, that first experience was definitely the scariest. Because I had no idea what was happening, I started really believing there was something wrong with me which made it all worse. Way worse.

Heart palpitations, chest pressure and tension, absence of sensation in my extremities, dizziness, and no breath. If you've ever had anxiety or panic, you know how frightening it is. You know that it feels like the end of your life.

Eventually I decided to go see a doctor. Three weeks of multiple appointments and many tests later, he gave me a prescription for Librium—that was the early 1980's version of current day psychoactive drugs like Xanax. It is designed to change the biochemistry, relax the muscles and turn off the mental chatter. Sadly, these types of drugs are now advertised on television as part of an everyday, normal lifestyle.

On screen: *A video of a happy couple playing with their kids, surrounded by family at a picnic in the park.* The voice over: "*Do you suffer from social anxiety? Then take this drug; all your troubles will disappear.*" *All is well.* And of course, there's the voice-under that speaks softly for three minutes about the dangers and side effects of these types of pharmaceuticals. The list is long.

And there is still a lack of education about potential alternatives and non-chemical solutions to pharmaceutical intervention for anxiety and panic.

In those days, there was no internet to look up symptoms and causes or information about medications, so I remained in the dark about my condition for some time. I can't even remember how I finally found out the name of my condition.

Well, the prescription was filled, though lucky for me I didn't use it. Something in me looked at that bottle and said, "what are you doing?" Instead, I stuffed it way back on the linen closet shelf, forgotten until I moved two years later. I never opened it.

Meanwhile though, I was still suffering through the ultimately waning numbers of many panic attacks which eventually stopped completely when I learned to ground and center.

A Magical Spiritual Adventure

One of the most intense of these experiences came on while sitting on a breakwall looking up at the Golden Gate Bridge.

It was a cold and foggy afternoon in 1987 when I worked my way through the minefield of a very severe panic attack. After 4 years of traditional counseling for stress and anxiety—my panic became very familiar territory, yet these episodes remained very frightening experiences.

That day, a woman I was working with stood by to help me back into my body. As I settled, she told me about a psychic studies program in Berkeley that would help me. She was calm and quite certain, so I asked very few questions, signed on for a reading and pretty immediately enrolled in a meditation for self-healing class.

Relax your Body, Quiet your Mind

Within two weeks the panic attacks disappeared! Two years later I finished four more six-week classes and an 18-month self-healing and clairvoyant training at Berkeley Psychic Institute (BPI). To this day, I continue my studies with the teachers who have committed their lives to this body of work, originally created by Lewis Bostwick.

As a sensitive and empathic person, learning to ground, find personal space and anchor my energy in my body gave me invaluable tools to live in the world. I was no longer preoccupied with the state of my body and able to progress spiritually.

Not only one of the most important decisions I've ever made for myself, this choice set the tone for my current life's work. It was key in redirecting me and re-integrating with my soul.

Some of us are naturally high-strung, potentially wired for stress and anxiety. Some of us are sensitive to the energy that roams human existence on this planet, finding it really difficult to match the frequency here. We were given no tools to navigate and integrate, so we gird our loins, fending off the experiences. Some of us are just ungrounded—maybe because we have trouble being here in the midst of all this chaos, maybe because we haven't acknowledged our choice to be spiritual entities living in the body. Others have experienced so much trauma in their lives, that disengaging or even dissociating from the the body is the only way to survive this life here.

Whatever the case or cause, it is our soul path or dharma to be embodied. It is a choice we made. We are here, that is obvious, no matter how painful or filled with anxiety it may be.

Healing may seem out of reach, as though it's way off in the distance, a huge challenge or even an impossibility. Maybe you've never thought about the potential for healing your stress or anxiety. From where you are now, in the context of your current choices, it just seems…well, it feels unattainable.

I hear you.

Did you know that anxiety is a sign of evolution? Yes; I discovered this a short while ago while coaching someone who had a lot of what she called anxiety. Over many months—actually a couple years, I realized she was describing the appearance and experience of emotions she had never acknowledged. Her lifelong beliefs were being challenged after she'd changed her lifestyle and living arrangement, which triggered the dissolution of beliefs she had held for 70 years or more.

When she started to "feel," after all this time, a stressful combination of fear and excitement added spice to the biochemical stew, and voila!, twice baked anxiety.

Without information and support, anxiety easily turns into panic. With knowledge though—the courage to feel what is, and the willingness to speak out loud the sensations and emotions that lie deep, we are provided just enough propulsion to bust through the glass ceiling between the false sense of safety and fear, to get to the next level.

This is true for all humans, not only those who have experienced panic.

When we are willing to express, rather than hide or avoid, we can break the lock and the cycle of self-suppression and ignorance. Depending on the individual and the situation, this process may need support from appropriate professionals and workable methods.

Maybe it's simply about making a different choice—a new choice that will open up territory you've never seen nor experienced before. This is a soul choice.

Welcome to your inner terrain.

Your adventure has just begun. With sincerity and a little discipline, your first stop is physical relaxation. When your nervous system calms down a little, the circular thoughts of your monkey mind begin to slow down and quiet a bit too. When that lower mind slows down you create an opportunity to meet your higher mind and the inspired thoughts of your soul's purpose.

And then there is the in-between place—snuggled into the crack separating the lower and inspired minds. When the crack widens, your emotions will begin to surface. This part of the journey is learning to witness and even experience the difficulties of feeling.

Collateral beauty does exist. Emotions are part of being human. When we say hello to them, allowing them to just be, they move through the body naturally and usually pretty quickly. When they flow, they don't have time to stir a lot of chemistry—the primary reason we are uncomfortable with emotions.

When you greet the emotions, acknowledging their message—now unblocked, they flow and are integrated into the experience. A memory is created without the chemical charge.

This choice has now just helped you begin to dissolve hardened patterns and traumatic responses. Soon you will naturally dislodge old beliefs and constructs, making lots more space to create different pictures and experiences.

Intention of this Book

Helping people with stress, anxiety, monkey-mind and panic. Helping people find a way inside. Helping people ask for what they want—to communicate, express and interact with their hidden and forgotten parts. Helping people to be responsible for themselves. This is the purpose of this book.

"Relax Your Body, Quiet Your Mind" is created with conscious rest and relaxation in mind, guiding people into experiencing a place of self-motivated restoration. It is created for anyone who experiences stress or any of the deeper sensations that spin into and out of stress.

Simple methods for effortless living, these practices are designed to provoke your felt senses, acknowledge your inner sight, enhance your awareness and your ability to create anything and everything you've ever dreamed.

Relax your Body, Quiet your Mind

Each week for the next year, we will focus on a different practice to center yourself in your body, your heart and your energy field. Let go. Remember, you are only truly able to change what happens within the space three feet around you. Enjoy the gentle, effortless place of rest, rejuvenation and recapitulation of your inner senses.

Learn to be ok with your thoughts, emotions and sensations. Love yourself as you are. You might just find yourself drifting into the deeper meditative states—the truly spiritual realm of your soul's domain.

Grateful for it all.

Michele

Health & Exercise Considerations

This book and the suggested practices are not intended to give nor replace medical care and professional health advice.

Even though the practices are mostly non-physical and gentle in nature, and can be performed by most people with positive results, some may be contra-indicated for certain conditions.

Please consult with your doctor or a professional health care advisor before practicing.

Introduction

Using this Book

This book is intended to be used as an annual, week by week guide to relaxing your body and quieting your mind. Each week presents one relaxation practice using conscious breath, gentle movement or a visualization. Sometimes the practice incorporates all three.

There are many options.

You may want to use these practices as intended, building one upon the next in a weekly sequence. If you are a visual person, you might want to add a deck of the *Sacred Body Cards* to enhance your experience with the practices here. If you are a contemplative person, you might want to add the *Sacred Body Cards'* original companion book of symbols, *"Sacred Body Wisdom."*

If you have the *Sacred Body Cards,* you can ask questions about your growth, drawing single cards to find a random practice assignment, or you can create spreads (found in the Maps & Spreads section of *"Sacred Body Wisdom"*) that point you down a specific path using multiple cards and related practices from this resource.

You can follow the practices as outlined, pulling the *Sacred Body Card* that fits the practice for each week adding a little dimension to your experience. You can follow this book alone or both books each week. You might also choose a more random and spontaneous way of interacting with the practices by simply opening to a page.

The Sacred Body Oracle & Cards

The oracle and cards combine *Sacred Body Cards* & *"Sacred Body Wisdom."* It is an oracle deck of awareness and practice, designed to help you connect your physical body to spirit through your *blueprint*, awakening and remembering the divine within you. There are 72 cards with 9 theme cards or *Sacred Gateways*, and 63 *Stepping Stones* in between the gates. As suggested, you can use this set in combination with *"Relax your Body, Quiet your Mind."*

Conscious Evolution

The *Sacred Gateways* open into different levels of awareness and consciousness. The *Stepping Stones* within them hold space for the themes of the *Sacred Gateways* and are the focus of this book.

Take a breath. Slow down. Breathe again. Take each step one at a time.

Sacred Body Oracle and Cards as well as this book: *"Relax your Body, Quiet your Mind,"* are about potential—your human potential to know yourself, to heal, grow and make changes; to transmit—simply by being, your wholeness, your divinity, your humanity and your affinity for yourself and others.

Relax your Body, Quiet your Mind

This oracle deck is designed to be inspirational and provocative, helping you evoke from within—self-inquiry and reflection, self-healing and mastery. Rather than answers, each card and its practices will ask you to consider new questions that will guide you down a path of self-discovery, through curiosity and discipline. You will evoke much from your unexplored inner terrain, reminding you how to transform knowledge to wisdom through practice, every day choices, and actions.

It's not the answers, but the questions that drive us to open the *Sacred Gateways* and penetrate the veils between the worlds.

The Journey

Conscious or not, when you begin to relax your body and quiet your mind, you have chosen to focus. It may be a deepening of an old adventure revisited, or a new path altogether. Either way, your journey can potentially begin at any point along the way, wherever you are in present time. With focus and intention, you can simply walk through the door that is open to you. Whether self-directed or in a pre-determined path, each card and its practice offer information related to your inquiry and intention.

Stay curious.

Practicing

Begin anytime of the year. These practices are based on the intention of 52-weeks in the order given over 12 months. Even so, your personal cycle could be 52 days, or in any way you choose to engage. Start when you feel compelled or committed and take them at your own pace.

There are suggested practices for each *Stepping Stone* and questions posed for self-reflection. A key part of the path, the *Windows to the Soul* theme is informational and passively supportive in this book. It is the *Sacred Gateway* where knowledge becomes wisdom through various disciplines or practices.

The eight windows and eight types of practice include: *Breath, Visualization, Energy Awareness, Movement, Energy Circulation, Self-Reflection, Witnessing, and Self-Mastery,* all of which are represented throughout this book in various forms—actual practices and supportive written passages. Some practices may seem to be repeats of a previous week, though they are actually building blocks that trigger deeper experiences using similar tools and visuals. Each practice builds upon the next, yet can be performed in any order, at any time as well.

And, though the practices are not always an exact match to their companions' messages from the cards, they are compliments to the oracular provocations. They will always play a role to correspond, respond, trigger, oppose and balance.

Evolution of Practice

Please keep in mind, these practices are deceptively simple.

If you only read the words, give them lip service, or in any way offer them only rote attention, they will remain superficial. It's all in the level of intention and sincerity—the way you perceive, approach and receive, that gives each practice its depth. More than that, it's really about what you hear—how you listen to your body and its felt senses that creates the depth in these storylines.

In your daily practice you will journey through nine *Sacred Gateways* that represent the evolving levels of consciousness, and 52 different practices (one for each week of the year) or *Stepping Stones*. As you progress, you will soon discover there are also three veils that separate the worlds: lower, middle, and upper worlds. Knowing where you are in the worlds, can open you to a deeper understanding of the practices along the way. Near the end of the year of practices (after week 44), you will reach the *Sacred Gateway* called *Windows to the Soul*. This is another learning stage about the different types of practice that readies you to move even further into your ability to focus and integrate, mastering the frequencies of each of the remaining practices.

Each of the 52 weekly practices has three components:

Center: Step One prepares the body-mind for what is to come. Calling your attention back to yourself in the beginning of each practice, it assists you in being present, expanding your felt sense, seeing clearly. and truly finding a state of relaxation. This is the most important aspect of the practice, and usually involves sitting or lying in a comfortable position and breathing consciously.

Relax your Body, Quiet your Mind

Be sure to create an environment in which you can easily find your center and rest. It may involve finding props—pillows, blankets, bolsters, eye covers, etc., to support your body in its most relaxed position.

There is a time before centering during which you may want to stimulate the circulation of blood and nerve energies. Counterintuitively, it may be more difficult to relax when your body has been inactive for some time.

Energy becomes stagnant, muscles tighten, blood pools and nerve messages blocked. If you were to lay down after being inactive or stagnant, your body might just twitch and wiggle—the restlessness overwhelming and very distracting. The solution is to move! There are a few exercises listed at the end of this section that will clear away the stagnancy and allow your body to settle in for some restoration: jiggle and shake, take a walk, stretch or even dance for a few minutes.

These movements will trigger the body's inherent wisdom to breathe naturally, and the breath will help you to release enough energy to find your way back into center. Each of the centering practices requests that you breathe naturally for a while to find your center; these pre-practices help you let "off steam" and get closer to that place inside yourself.

Centering gives you a place to begin; a place from which you are capable of managing energy more expeditiously; a place to release the old, creating space for the new.

Relax your Body, Quiet your Mind

Relax: Step Two is the core part of the practice, and the time you actually spend in relaxation. It doesn't mean there are no thoughts or sensations. In fact, at first you are likely to be even more aware of your felt senses. Ideally you stay awake and aware, which helps you to stay conscious as you transition through the brainwave levels and one day even sensory withdrawal.

Without agenda or effort, relaxation is truly an intentional practice. Eventually, the practice entrains you to be more relaxed in your daily living experiences.

Practices are many and varied, sometimes physical, sometimes visual, and they always focus on the breath. Uncomplicated by the need to change something, the relaxation practice often calls you to be aware of your current state and then to release it.

Releasing energy is something you will often do in those moments. And rather than shifting everything right then, it is more about creating an environment or a platform for change in your daily life—before and after your practice. Releasing during practice isn't necessarily a permanent solution. It simply allows you to take a moment to recognize and feel yourself in present time, to accept that state, being with the sensation or emotion for a short time, and then letting it go in practice.

Actualizing in daily life is the real litmus test for your practices.

Relaxation is not intended to mesmerize or put you into a trance state. The intention of these practices is to train and entrain you to stay conscious and aware; to feel your body, not

Relax your Body, Quiet your Mind

ignore it. Sometimes you will feel a lot and have heightened awareness of many sensations—both new and familiar. Sometimes you will feel nothing. It's important not to judge your experience as better because you have no sensation or more awareness when you do feel. Neither is more advanced than another.

You may feel energized, soft, sleepy, inspired, excited, pressured, thoughtful, emotional, and many other possibilities. Human conditioning often overrides emotions and sensation, so here you will often focus on what you feel and how you perceive those feelings. The point of relaxing is first to feel and be aware—to break through your self-created "numbness to function" state. At some point, relaxation becomes about something entirely different—a lowered yet still conscious brainwave state, retention of the senses and a depth of awareness beyond feeling.

Try not to get caught in the definitions or phenomenon of the moment. Just allow it to be.

Integrate: In Step Three you slowly come out of your relaxation, becoming more aware of your body in space. Be still and just notice for a few moments. Then move into a little self-inquiry and contemplation. An inspiration or provocative idea is presented for your consideration and awareness.

Healing and progress happens during those moments of integration.

Relax your Body, Quiet your Mind

Things to Keep in Mind when Practicing

Although quite gentle, some of the movement practices may be contraindicated for your personal condition. Please move only in a range that is comfortable for your body, and always consult with your health care professional before attempting any new exercise, whether passive or active.

1. Be gentle with yourself, aware of your current state of mind and body.

2. If you are uncertain about a specific practice, consult your inner guidance or your health care professional to see if it is appropriate for your current state of health and well-being.

3. None of these exercises will harm you if done thoughtfully and slowly, and none of them are intended to replace needed medical attention. *Please consult with your doctor or health care advisor before practicing any new exercises.*

4. Repeat each exercise within the practice 3x, 6x, or 9x. As you advance, you may build repetition if you like, in the same increments.

5. Practice assists you in becoming aware of yourself in deeper ways by anchoring your energy in your body and taking ownership of your personal space.

6. Not all practices suggested are designed to be solely meditative. If you were to walk the path of the cards in the order of their

prescribed evolution, you would practice in relation to that order by:

Sensing: Organic Body, The Elements
Feeling: Sacred Cisterns, Rivers & Streams
Visualizing: Soul to Soul
Experiencing: The Mystical Journey, Gateways to the Heights
Being: Unity

7. This book offers a more in-depth and detailed version of the same practices for each card listed in *"Sacred Body Wisdom: Mystical Conversations Between Body & Spirit."*

Common Relaxation Practices

-*Conscious Breathing:* can be a simple awareness practice that follows the path of the breath; or it might encourage you to create various breathing patterns with specific instructions.

-*Contemplation & Inquiry:* thinking or reflecting about the meaning of something; speaking with oneself through the inner voice.

-*Light & Sound Frequencies:* often combined to slowly lower brainwaves from stress to rest in the form of music and hertz driven sound frequencies.

-*Meditation:* sitting in stillness, *simple quiet time,* waiting, allowing images or relaxed states to appear; slowing down to enhance awareness.

Relax your Body, Quiet your Mind

-*Restorative Yoga:* supports and assists the body in reaching a relaxed state—thoughts recede and the mind becomes quiet.

-*Savasana:* often equated with Restorative and Nidra yogas as well as the ending pose in most active yoga classes. Translated as corpse pose, its intention is rest and restoration. It is used as a quiet time that can be a stand alone practice or integrated into all others.

-*Singular Focus:* focus, holding an image or sacred symbol in your mind's eye.

-*Visualization:* use of mental imagery or a core shamanic journey to relax or explore the inner realms; can be guided or self-directed; listening to scripted, relaxing music, word or sounds.

-*Yoga Nidra:* also known as yoga sleep, takes you down through the levels of physical, mental and emotional relaxation, until you reach the bridge between alpha and theta brainwaves, sometimes deeper.

Physical Body Relaxation & Preparation for Stillness

Many of the blocks to relaxation are found in physical sensation: the desire to get up and move, body twitches, emotional chemistry and general irritability. Getting beyond this could be as simple as standing up and jiggling or shaking the body to release excess energy. These practices are also stand alone for circulation, release, balance and accumulation of physical energies.

Relax your Body, Quiet your Mind

Remember to consult with your doctor or health care advisor before practicing any new exercises.

-Tapping: palm patting all over the body for circulation and balancing
-Vibrating: gentle jiggling & shaking
-Tai Chi & Qi Gong
-Stretching & slow, gentle movements: like rolling, swaying; finding natural inner rhythm
-Meditative or contemplative walking (not hiking nor strenuous)

Elements of Stress

"Anxiety was born in the very same moment as mankind. And since we will never be able to master it, we will have to learn to live with it, just as we have learned to live with the storms," from the "*Manuscript Found in Accra*," by Paulo Coelho.

Our Bodies Reflect Our Environment

More so most recently, our planet works overtime, flinging elemental energies around wildly as she expresses her stress and power. Stern and loud, her voice speaks to us about our own rouge expressions, reflecting back the chaos within our human beingness. She not only asks us to handle more and more external change as our cells re-call the ancient ways and how then, we acknowledged our lack of control over the elements. She also begs us to transform our inner terrain, and when we don't have ears to hear, we feel the roar of her soul vibrating through our bones.

Relax your Body, Quiet your Mind

Whether planetary or not, stress is elemental; it's built into our human design, residing deep within the bones of our DNA. We're programmed with both the ability to respond to and create stress as an integral part of our nervous system.

On an unconscious level, our bodies react to situations through our sensory perceptions which trigger the autonomic nervous system, endocrine and immune systems. Although this stress response is primarily out of our control, we can install practices to train our minds to be quieter and teach our bodies to relax in practice which entrains us to perform in situ.

On a more adaptive and sometimes conscious level, stress is the hot, red, reactive, efferent impulse of control and desire for power over our environment—internal and external. At times a bit quieter and more productive, it's the active, masculine side of our genetic make-up. Both male and female bodies have this energetic and physiological construct.

We can actually regulate these types of responses through changes in attitude, management of thought and emotion, applied to learned, new behaviors. In a way, we are taming the sympathic dominance of our autonomic nervous system.

And someplace inside us all, there is a witness who sits in a central, neutral balance point. And no matter what is happening *out there* or *in here,* that witness can find acceptance for it all.

This is the feminine, receptive side of our human construct.

When we reach into the reflective aspects of ourselves, we are calling on the parasympathetic branch of the autonomic nervous system for balance.

Why do we Stress?

Many of us actually like stress because it's in our nature to push the envelope. There is a fine line between expanding and blowing out at the seams. The talent is knowing just how far and in what ways we can push ourselves for purposes of learning and growing before "it" truly becomes a stress monster or even an addiction.

The energy of our human composite is something akin to creation and destruction, expansion and contraction, permeability and boundaries, masculine and feminine principles. These are the foundations from which we incorporate stress for natural evolution, though in this era we sometimes push our minds and bodies so far with the constant pressure of the media and the introduction of newer and grander technologies, we fry our brains and injure our constitutions.

If we were a bit more curious, as opposed to distracted and compulsive, maybe we wouldn't be quite so stressed. Then again, maybe we would be bored from a lack of polarity.

It's in us to be a little stressed, and if we aren't already naturally and actively engaged in the practice of stress, we make it so, everywhere we go. We sometimes wear stress like a trophy in every season by resisting what we've already chosen–human form, earth life, our families, jobs and more.

This resistance runs deep. On the outside it may look a lot like certainty, knowingness, intelligence and actualization, especially when we look at ourselves in the mirror. Our minds see what they want to see.

Yet, when we're brave enough to slow down and see more clearly—enough to experience a different rhythm—an internal rhythm, one linked to the rhythms and tides of our planet and beyond—then we can feel that there just might be something *"off"* inside of us. Until we change our pace for a mere moment, until we live without extreme stress and breathe a bit more consciously, we'll never know this other option exists.

It's also in us to be free and relaxed, if only we could trust and allow the Sun to shine, the winds to blow, the earth to quake and the rains to pour without our help and interference. If we did allow it, if we did use our will coupled with clear thought and inspiration, we could use our God-given gifts to manifest anything, anytime.

So the practice—the most balanced attitude we can play into the world—is acceptance and gratitude. Would you like to feel yourself more deeply…knowing yourself enough to make a change?

First you need to learn how to breathe and feel your body.

Relax your Body, Quiet your Mind

Anatomy and Energy of Relaxation

The Autonomic Nervous System
The Autonomic Nervous System (ANS) is where our stress vs. relaxation responses originate—physiologically speaking, and it's part of our body-spirit communication mechanism.

One of the first systems to develop in utero, the ANS has two parts: the sympathetic branch which triggers the *fight or flight* impulse and mobilizes resources to act under stress; and the parasympathetic branch which activates our natural capacity for relaxation, digestion, regulation of internal organs and anything that happens while the body is at *rest*.

Since the human body is equipped with two facets of the ANS, we utilize both in concert with one another, and need both to survive. Even so, most people become dominant in one or the other.

In simple terms, here's the way our system expresses stress: we perceive a potentially dangerous situation and the forebrain transmits this information to the hypothalamus deep in the midbrain. The hypothalamus sends a message via the sympathetic (masculine, Yang, Sun) branch of the ANS to the endocrine system (pituitary, adrenals) which then pumps up the appropriate chemicals to move the limbs and manage the danger. In the end, it's usually adrenalin that rules our systems, making us feel fast, strong and powerful, able to overcome anything. It's also the panic hormone. So we run away, or we stand and take on the challenge. This is better known as *fight or flight* and it takes us back to our reptilian patterns.

Energetic Anatomy

In energetic terms, the ANS mirrors our masculine and feminine energies. We can also see them represented in Hermes' staff of Aesclepion entwined by two serpents—the staff is the spinal column or subtle body central channel, and the serpents represent the two branches of the ANS or secondary subtle channels. Altogether, they form the physiology of the central nervous system, and in subtle terms, they are the three primary nadis—energy channels transporting prana from centerline into the subtle body matrix.

Nadis are energetic rivers or channels through which subtle energies flow. There are three main subtle channels: Sushumna is the central channel and is reflected physically as the spinal column; Ida and Pingala relate to the ANS as positive and negative, active and receptive, masculine and feminine energies. Feminine energy is lunar, cool, silver or blue, receptive, shadowy and is associated with Ida; while Pingala, the masculine energy, is hot, red or gold, light, active, and solar.

In Taoism, these same two lines are commonly known as Yin and Yang energies. All meridian channels have Yin or Yang designations.

Whatever the metaphor, we operate in a constant active and receptive dance throughout our day. Everything is set up for perfect cyclical rhythms.

We already know that all facets of beingness influence one

another. Imbalance on any level is stressful for the human physiology, the emotional and mental constitution, as well as spiritually.

The key is balance and integration—the integration of masculine and feminine principles, using our energy properly and appropriately, in the moment. This is natural law—the law of energy.

Relief and Resolution

Stress can be addressed from any level and create results on all others. For example, we can find a way to slow our minds which could be an effective remedy for emotional distress, physical tension and spiritual or energetic integration.

Or, we can engage in a physical restorative yoga practice to effect change in the emotional, mental and spiritual realms as well. With any immersion, there are always varying depths of exploration and need for consistent practice and attention, especially if the stress is environmental, unmanageable and chronic.

There are many different methods for stress relief, management and reduction. Training is learning in practice. Entrainment is the body's ability to perform in situ based on these learned skills. This concept is akin to the difference between knowledge and wisdom. Knowledge is information gathered, wisdom is experience gained from the knowledge that is gathered.

The practices listed here will take you step by step, into the softer

Relax your Body, Quiet your Mind

quiet of inner realms, inside your personal inner kingdom where you are able to perceive all facets of your incredible existence. Rather than being at the effect of those experiences, you simply accept them and become an empowered witness.

All this said—in the roux you'll find the grit and the glue. Much more than a correction, it's an alchemical blend: the grit is accepting who you are; the glue is its embrace.

Feel your body. It unlocks the door to everything.

Definitions

The practice instructions include many terms which may warrant some definition. Here is a simple description of each of these concepts. They are easily searchable online if you'd like more information about these, or you may have your own information about them already.

-*Afference*: energy that moves into center

-*Akashic Records:* soul memory, eternal knowledge encoded on the spiritual planes available through psychic means

-*Apana*: downward or outward moving pranic energy, aids release of stagnancy—physically and energetically

-*Aura:* energy field, electromagnetic field

-*Awareness:* realization, perception, consciousness

-*Cauldrons:* a container for energy; each cauldron holds 1-2 chakras; three primary energy centers related to subtle bodies: lower abdomen, chest, and neck-head region

-*Center:* as in center of head, centerline, and center of your aura; an important aspect of preparation for relaxation. In fact, the human glandular and nervous systems cannot be consciously relaxed if your attention and awareness are off center, outside, or following thoughts and events from the past or worrying about the future

-*Center of the aura* is the centered relationship between your physical body and its energy field

-*Center of head* is exactly that: the space exactly centered in between your head bones on all sides

-*Centerline* is the relationship between head and tail or feet in a physical context. It runs down the spinal column in the middle of the body. In a subtle body context, it relates to the line between the crown and root chakras which are housed in the central channel

-*Central Channel:* centerline; also see pranic tube, shushumna

-*Chakra:* an energy center in the subtle anatomy linked to the physical body through various subtle energy channels and related subtle bodies; wheels of energy anchored in the subtle body (blueprint) central channel, mirroring the spinal column and nerve plexi

Common names for chakras— root, sacral, solar, heart, throat, third eye and crown, are given to the primary chakras to identify their location in the human body

-*Chi*: life force; see prana

-*Cisterns:* cauldrons

-*Clairaudience:* ability to hear spirit beyond the veils of the 3rd dimensional world

-Clairsentience: sympathy, ability to feel another's pain or physical sensation; differs from empathy

-Clairvoyance: clear sight, inner sight, psychic or soul sight, ability to see spirit

-Conscious: existing in a state of regular awareness; related to upper brain and frontal lobe

-Cosmic Energy: divine, universal or heavenly energy

-Dichotomy: two sides of the same coin or structure creating opposing parts

-Efference: energy moving away from center

-Empathy: ability to feel another's emotions; ability to interact from higher emotions and change the frequency of a shared space merely by being present there

-Energy Field: electromagnetic field, aura

-Etheric Body: a subtle body, KA body, pranic body, the blueprint

-Feel or feelings: not emotional, but physical unless referred to as emotions

-Felt Sense: feelings; the awareness of the physical and energetic sensations; chemical responses the body produces to manage the inner and outer environments

-*Flower of Life:* sacred geometrical shape of multiple conjoined circles; contains the fundamentals of spiritual life

-*Gateway:* a passageway and is related to a chakra, yet more importantly it is an evolutionary point. In yoga it is called a *granthi* or knot, something to be untied as part of a progression or growth process

-*Gland*: like the pineal, pituitary, thyroid, thymus, ovaries, testes, adrenals; glands comprise the endocrine system which excretes hormones into the rest of the body for proper functioning on all levels. Each endocrine gland can be linked to a chakra energy

-*Granthi:* a spiritual knot which needs to be untied to enter and pass through a gateway

-*Hologram for the Divine*: everything holds imprints of the source

-*Human Torus:* self-perpetuating energy originating from within the pranic tube or central channel, circulating through the subtle and physical bodies, and into the auric field

-*Ida:* feminine energy line; parasympathetic branch of the autonomic nervous system; see also *Pingala*

-*Inner Kingdom:* sanctuary, center of head; pituitary, pineal, thalamus & hypothalamus glands; all link to the Big Dipper & the Polestar (North Star) through the crown of the head

-*Kundalini*: liquid golden light, subtle body energy, potent life force, cerebral spinal fluid

-*Lower World:* World of rebirth and transformation; see Upper and Middle Worlds

-*Meridians:* longitudinal masculine and feminine energy lines and connections between acupressure points; subtly defined in the blueprint and fascia of the physical body and also in the energy field as related to the elements and the cosmos

-*Middle World*: human world and the world of nature spirits; see Lower and Upper Worlds

-*Nadis:* subtle energy channels

-*Pelvic Bowl:* the lower abdomen

-*Pelvic Floor:* soft tissues between the four bony pelvic points: pubic, tail and sitting bones

-*Pentacle*: five-pointed star symbolizing the five elements

-*Pingala:* masculine energy line, sympathetic branch of the autonomic nervous system; see also *Ida*

-*Plexus*: as in Solar Plexus, indicates the general location of a chakra. Physically speaking, a plexus is a network of blood vessels and nerves which exit the spinal column and ultimately follow a common pathway through the physical body into the extremities and organs. Energetically speaking, the chakra plexi also circulate energies (like blood), and electrical impulses (like nerves), through nadis (channels). These channels are conduits that run through the subtle bodies (which are over and underlays) and also affect the physical body. Like the seven body chakras, there are seven nerve-blood plexi in the human body.

-*Polarity*: magnetics, opposite energies

-*Prana*: inward or upward moving life force, nourishment

-*Pranic Tube:* central channel; prana flows through it

-*Pre-cognition:* before cognition; foresight, ability to know before something happens

-*Psychometry:* seeing or sensing through the hands

-*Qabala:* Tree of Life as adopted by Western Esotericism-Mysticism

-*Rose:* sacred flower symbolizing the depth of relationship, growth and spiritual essence

-*Sacred Spiral:* a singular spiral or vortex of energy

-*Sensation:* refers to your physical experience of both internal and external, provoked and evoked, stimuli. See felt sense

-*Shushumna:* central channel or pillar, pranic tube, central nervous system

-*Six-Pointed Star:* a symbol of heaven embodied, or body opening to spirit. As Above, So Below

-*Subconscious:* related to what lies underneath the conscious mind or thoughts; midbrain, emotions and bio-chemistry

-*Subtle Body:* a system of subtle energies related to the human form. Essentially there are three primary bodies related to the human experience: physical (gross/human), mental-emotions (subtle/energy), and information, wisdom or intellect (causal/spiritual), depending upon which doctrines or acculturations are used. The energy/subtle body has seven levels or lesser subtle forms we also call subtle bodies

-*Triple Spiral* (Celtic): three linked spirals symbolizing land, sea and sky; or body, mind-emotion and spirit

-*Triquetra:* sacred Celtic trinity symbol

-*Unconscious*: information that is stored, or repressed states of being, held in a state of non-regular awareness, unknown; lower brain

-*Upper World:* spirit world; see Lower & Middle Worlds

-*Vitruvian Man:* (DaVinci) proportional human form as connected to the elements and the cosmos

Relax your Body, Quiet your Mind

-*Wheel of Life*: seasonal wheel of cycles; directions, elements, and existence

Weekly Relaxation Practices

*Through the sacred gateways of consciousness and evolution,
your journey is spiritual in intention, energetically driven,
and human in nature.*

Your body is your companion.
The Organic Body

Natural law your foundation.
The Elements

Your witness awakens in center.
Sacred Cisterns

Merging energy and physiology.
Rivers & Streams

Gifts of soul are remembered.
Soul to Soul

The tree of life opens the way.
The Mystical Journey

Relax your Body, Quiet your Mind

Practice is your propulsion.
Windows to your Soul

Divine energy infuses every cell.
Gateways to the Heights

The home light burns eternal.
Unity

The Organic Body
Birth

Your body is a master alchemist, offering you numinous gifts of feeling. The wind breezing through your hair; rain dropping gently on your face; flames of solar passion in your heart; warm sand yielding under your feet; an etheric mantle covering your skin.
Enjoy the physical sensations, remembering, deep inside there are many kindred and even subtler forms awakening greater experiences.

Are you looking at your health and wellbeing in a solely physical manner or do you find ways to expand your health and well being into and beyond what you can see or touch?

Relax your Body, Quiet your Mind

The Mystic's Journey

The *Sacred Gateway* of the *Organic Body* opens with the merger of your parents seeds, takes you through the womb time, your first breath and into early life. It synchronizes with your energy field; awakening and filling the body, moving through its every cell and anchors fully as you embrace the divine within. The *Organic Body* theme unfolds in the 1st wisdom ring at the beginning of life on earth. Once through the *Sacred Gateway*, there are 5 *stepping stones* of evolution in this theme.

1
Respiration

Air

The Eastern winds of spirit blow through your body, provoking you to meet its rhythms as your awareness dances with inspiration.
Lie on your back, close your eyes and breathe.

Notice where you feel the wind blowing across your skin. Notice the breath of spirit as you breathe deeply, in and then out again.

How does your body feel when you breathe consciously?

Relax your Body, Quiet your Mind

Center

Receive the winds of inspiration through your breath.

Take a few moments for yourself and just breathe. Find a comfortable position, close your eyes and breathe naturally for a while. Let your bones sink into gravity with each exhalation; your muscles slowly soften. Be here until you feel centered in your body.

Relax: *Receptive Breath*

-Notice any sensation as your breath moves freely through you.

-Place your hands on your body to connect more deeply with your body's ability to receive your breath.

-Be here for a while, feeling the breath in your body.

-Now begin to notice where your breath feels limited—anyplace your body is tense, even rigid; any place your breath may feel blocked.

-Try not to force anything, instead becoming more aware of the sensation in these unreceptive places.

-Continue to breathe, using your breath to explore the sensation in your body.

-Your bones become even heavier with each exhalation. Be here for a while, easing your breath through your body.

Integrate

Just breathe. You are here, now. Feel your resistance begin to soften, as the tightness begins to melt. Now you can receive the parts of you that were forgotten behind the screen of resistance.

2
Digestion

Fire

Fire is the light, the alchemical wand of spirit transforming you from the inside out. It metabolizes emotions, thoughts, the overloads of everyday life, old habits and programming. Feel the warmth of the Sun in your belly.

Expand your belly as you inhale, relaxing your muscles as you exhale.

Will you create a space in your belly to digest your stagnant energies?

Relax your Body, Quiet your Mind

Center

Feel the fires of transformation deep in your belly.

Lie on your back, close your eyes and just breathe as you settle in to rest. Place your hands on your belly, allowing them to rise as you inhale and fall as you exhale. Breathe and feel your belly expanding and contracting, softening, bone by bone, muscle by muscle. Be here until you feel centered.

Relax: *Belly Breath*

-Continue to breathe—expanding and contracting, your belly button dropping deep into your lower belly as you exhale, rising toward the ceiling as you inhale. Be with this breath cycle for some time.

-Next, feel your breath filling your upper belly, opening the front of your ribs as you inhale, softening them down into your belly as you exhale. Be with this breath cycle for some time.

-Now feel your breath filling the whole space inside your belly—upper and lower. Expand your whole belly like a balloon as you inhale, deflating the balloon as you exhale. Be with this breath cycle for some time.

-Rest here for a few minutes, feeling the breath move through your body as your belly rises and falls, effortlessly following your natural rhythms.

Integrate

Just breathe. You are here now. Your digestive fires are stoked with each breath inward, burning away the dross of the past, spinning the colorful threads of present time.

3
Circulation

Water

Water transmutes emotions, carrying them from the unconscious and subconscious realms into consciousness and release. Imagine your body filled with the waters of purification—three shimmering pools of energy that overflow with emotions. Shake up your energy and feel the sediment flowing from the unconscious realms into consciousness and finally release.

Do you feel a sense of clarity as your energy circulates?

Relax your Body, Quiet your Mind

Center

Feel the waters of purification gently lapping on the shores of your unconscious mind.

Cozy up quietly in a comfortable chair with your feet on the floor. Close your eyes and breathe naturally for a while, bringing your attention in from the outside world. Be here until you feel more centered.

Relax: *Pooling Breath*

-Breathe through your nose into the center of your head, allowing the breath to swirl gently, clearing away thoughts and emotions of days gone by.

-As you exhale, allow the stagnant energy to stream down through your centerline into the core of the earth. Be with this breath as long as you like.

-Now feel your breath pooling in the center of your head as you inhale. As you exhale the breath flows out of your head, down through your centerline into earth's core.

-Inhale again, feeling your breath pooling in your chest. As you exhale, the breath streams down through your centerline into the center of the earth.

-Inhale one more time, feeling your breath pooling in your belly and pelvis. As you exhale, feel your breath flowing down into the center of the planet.

-Pool your breath in all three locations—one by one.

-Be still for a while, breathing naturally, feeling your body, noticing your emotions, your thoughts and any physical sensations.

Integrate

Just breathe. You are here now. The waters of purification flow through you, dancing over rocky internal landmarks, streaming and gently cleansing, enlivening your body.

4
Restoration

Earth

Gently play your body drum to call forth your deepest healing alchemy—the vitality spring deep in the red well of bone marrow and its eternal stream of blood cells.

Can you feel the subtle fizzing sensation in your bones?

Relax your Body, Quiet your Mind

Center

Feel the call of the earth's heart beating in rhythm with your own.

Make a nest of blankets and pillows. Lie in the nest on your back, and close your eyes. Breathe naturally and gently, following your breath into your body. Notice any sensation as the breath moves in and out. Just be here for a while, feeling and connecting with the breath in your body.

Relax: *Connected Breath*

- Begin to gently and intentionally, direct your breath into your lower belly.
- Place your hands on your belly and feel the breath—the rise and fall of your belly under your hands. Just be here for a while, feeling the breath building in your belly.
- Now place one hand on your chest, leaving the other hand on your belly and breathe for a while.
- Inhale into your belly, then exhale that breath into your chest and ribcage. Next, inhale to your chest, then exhale into your belly. Inhale again, into your belly, repeating the cycle.
- Play with this breath cycle a few times, gently moving the breath between your chest and belly.
- Allow your breath to carve a path, creating a direct link between any two places in your body—intentionally connecting and sharing the breath, feeling the energy moving deep in your bones.

Integrate

Just breathe. You are here now. Feel your own breath, in-sync with the breath of the planet. Earth cradles you and supports your body's natural restorative cycles, strengthening you from deep within your bones.

5
Communication

Ether

When you open your body to the rhythms of spirit, you encourage your mind and heart through your inner voice. Sense the space around you, your body, the space around your body. Sense the room and the space of the room. Find yourself inside these spaces.

Are you in the center of your own space?

Relax your Body, Quiet your Mind

Center

Feel the particles of energy all around you, more subtle than the dust in a beam of sunlight.

Sit or lie comfortably. Feel your breath moving through your body. Create a grounding connection between your root and the center of the planet, sitting quietly as you gradually come into center.

Breathe fully into your body. Breathe into the space three feet around you. Feel the warmth of your breath, filling your body and the space around you.

Relax: *Your Energy Field*

- As your breath moves into the space around you, reach out with your hands to its outer edge.
- Notice how it feels to your touch, how far away its outer edge is from your body. The inner edge rests on your skin and the outer edge is about arms-length away from your body.
- Notice the space above, below, front, back, and around the sides. This is your personal energy field or aura.
- Notice how you feel when you compress and pull your aura in closer around your body.
- Notice how you feel when you fully expand it into the room. Bring your aura to a comfortable place around your body. Breathe to fill your personal space.

Integrate

Just notice. You are here now. Breathe naturally for a while, feeling your body and your aura. Breathe to nourish your body and fully own your personal space—your body and your aura.

Lower World

Realm of Rebirth

LOWER WORLD

Going within, you slide down the root system of the ancient tree giants, into the underworld where magic is born, across the mystical sea, in the lands of Avalon, Faery, Lemuria and the isles that have disappeared beyond the mists into the higher dimensions.

Can you smell, feel, touch or hear the life deep underground?
Can you imagine it?
How does it feel?

Relax your Body, Quiet your Mind

Practice: Sit next to your favorite tree, merging your trunk with the tree trunk. Imagine your body is linked to the root bed, into the magical worlds below, deep in Earth's center. Rather than a weekly practice, this is intended to set a tone for the next many weeks of your journey.

Once you've passed through several other gateways, you will arrive next at the veil of the middle world.

The Mystic's Journey
Explore the fantastic world of inner earth—your connection to the planet and the heartfelt beings who have evolved for thousands of years. They hold dear all the stories and frequencies of higher consciousness so that you might find your way to eternal life. They await your arrival.

The Elements

Cardinal Alchemy

Your personal essence is an expression of the Earth's seasonal rhythms and cycles, an allegory of nature's imprint in the DNA of all things. Its elemental texture weaves through your health and healing journey, connecting the dots between breath and inspiration; blood and the tides; digestion and wisdom; the still-strength in your bones, and the generation of eternal life force.

Can you feel the elements in your body?
Where do you feel most sensation?

Relax your Body, Quiet your Mind

The Mystic's Journey
The *Sacred Gateway* of *The Elements* theme opens first to inspiration in the east. Then it transports you into transformation in the south, cleansing in the west, and finally into restoration in the north at winter. Ride the elemental wave into the womb of the Earth Mother taking time for inner reflection and remembrance of the earthly and heavenly energies flowing through all things. Last, it moves into the integrated state of everything above is reflected below. The *Elements* theme unfolds in the 2nd wisdom ring, at the second level on the evolutionary path. Through the 5 elemental *Stepping Stones*, your etheric link to nature and the elements shows you the incredible power you have within it. This is natural law.

6
Eastern

Wind

Stand in the East where the wind clears away the dross, making space to begin anew. Relax now, breathing softly into the back of your throat, listening to the sounds of the wind inside the tunnel in your throat, waiting to be reborn into the light of Spring.

How can you use your breath to clear your internal environment?

Relax your Body, Quiet your Mind

Center

Like the blustery winds of Springtime, your breath clears away the intensity of charged energies, carrying you into this moment, away from the stickiness of that which no longer serves.

Lie on your back swathed in a blanked and begin to breathe naturally. Feel the effortlessness of the breath and the gentle way your body begins to relax inside your cocoon.

Feel the breath making its way through your body, filling every cell. Feel the breath moving into your nose as you inhale, and down your spine as you exhale. Be with this sensation for a while, just breathing and centering.

Relax: *Sounds of the Sea*

-Now, as you exhale, create a gentle sound in the back of your throat—a little bit like soft snoring.

-Be with this for some time, focusing on the sensation and the sound of that gentle breeze as the breath passes between your nasal passage and throat.

-As you settle into a place just on the edge of sleep, repeat 9 breaths in, 9 breaths out; feel the wind in your throat tunnel as you exhale.

Integrate

Just Breathe. You are here now. This is Ujjayi, calling forth the sounds of the wind and sea inside, deepening your connection to your core, your energy centers and your body's natural rhythms.

7

Southern

Sun

Facing south, dance in the streams of the Sun's golden rays as they warm your skin, open your heart and nourish your enthusiasm. Find the courage of your fire within to destroy the old as you create anew.

How can you use your inner fire to alchemize internal energies and more fully embrace the spirit inside?

Relax your Body, Quiet your Mind

Center

Feel the heat of alchemy's fiery wand, purging your body of dissonance, exposing the soul inside.

Sit upright in a chair with your feet on the floor. Close your eyes and go within, breathing naturally for a while. Breathe consciously, calling your attention in from the outside world until your body feels comfortable and your mind slows down any amount.

Relax: *Golden Suns*

-Imagine a golden ball of energy above your head, shining down around you like the Sun. Feel its brilliant golden glory warming your body.

-This is your Sun—a very special Sun. In fact, this Sun reflects the energy of your soul's highest creative essence. It also magnetizes and collects your personal energy from all the people and places you've recently visited.

-When the Sun has finished gathering your energy, invite it fully into your body, feeling it fill you from head to toes, through your arms and fingers.

-Feel the Sun filling your aura from overhead to the bottom under your feet. Feel it filling you from front to back and the sides of your energy field.

-Be still and breathe. Be with this sensation for several breaths.

Integrate

Just notice. You are here now. Feel your body inside the light and warmth of the fire within you—the energy of your Sun. Use your Sun every day to call back any energy you left out in the world.

8
Western
Sea

Facing west, imagine you are standing at the edge of the sea, sensing the gentle pull of the waves, the sand dissolving and disappearing from under your feet.
Gently ebbing tides carry you out across the sea of purification. Allow your breath to follow the rhythms of the tides, pooling in your heart.

Can you use the sea inside to alchemize your emotions?

Relax your Body, Quiet your Mind

Center

Your body's rhythms—its breath and cerebral spinal fluid, are in tune with the rhythms of the spin of the earth on its axis, the Milky Way Galaxy, and the sea inside.

Find a comfortable place to lie down on your back. Breathe naturally for a while until you center and settle, allowing gravity to anchor you in present time.

Relax: *Ocean Waves*

-Imagine you are floating on your back in the warm waters of a tropical sea. The Full Moon shines brilliantly in the dark night sky. Close your eyes and feel the support of the water underneath you.

-Your body moves with the gentle roll of the waves—in toward shore and out again. Rocking and relaxing as you breathe deeply, the sea lulls you inward.

-Synchronized with the natural rhythms of our planet and other celestial bodies in our galaxy equals in-synch with your personal inner rhythms and less stress.

-Breathe in and breathe out, synchronizing with the action of the waves.

Integrate

Just notice. You are here now. Attune to the essential and intimate conversation with your essence when you surrender to the rhythms of nature—the tide and currents within.

9
Northern

Cave

Face north and sense your body under the cloak of darkness—
deep in the cavern of the energy field around you,
quietly waiting to emerge into the light.
Rest, rejuvenate and grow in the quiet safety of nature's womb.

How can you use earth energy to break free of the old
and integrate the new?

Relax your Body, Quiet your Mind

Center

Your grounding is a conduit for clearing and transmuting stagnant energies; your breath directs them.

Sit in a comfortable upright posture with your feet on the floor. Your eyes are closed. Breathe naturally for a bit as you call yourself into center. Be here for a while breathing, releasing and centering.

Relax: *Grounding*

-Breathe into the center of your head through your nose, and exhale down your spinal column into the center of the Earth.

-Allow the breath to clear the center of your head as you inhale, releasing stagnant energies as you exhale.

-Imagine a connection between your root (tail bone area) and the center of the Earth. It may look like an actual root or a tree trunk. Be creative—it's your personal link between your body and the Earth's core.

-This is your grounding tube.

-Give it a tug on both ends to secure the connections. Focus on releasing any old or foreign energies, as you exhale down through your grounding into the center of the Earth.

-Be still. Be aware of your grounding. Continue breathing and releasing.

Integrate

Just notice. You are here now. Breathe and be with this for a while, feeling your body as it releases unwanted energies, restoring itself to its natural state of harmony and balance.

10
As Above So Below

Heaven & Gaia

Spirit is reflected in body and body in spirit. Breathe in a beam of golden light, connecting heaven to earth through your body. Feel it moving between your head and tail.

How is heaven and earth reflected inside you?

Relax your Body, Quiet your Mind

Center

Your your inner kingdom is the seat of your wisdom.

Sit in an upright posture, aligned yet comfortable. Your eyes are closed, your feet are on the floor, and your hands rest in your lap.

Begin breathing in through your nose and out through your mouth several times, letting go of stagnant energies. Then close your mouth and begin to breathe in and out through your nose. Be here for several breaths, noticing how you feel.

Relax: *The Center of your Head*

-Inhale through your nose into the center of your head, and exhale down the length of your spine.

-Repeat this cycle several times, allowing the breath to clear out the center of your head, releasing any sticky emotions, thoughts and beliefs as you exhale.

-Breathe, and breathe some more, diving deeper as more space opens in the center of your head.

-Notice how you feel as you settle into this very personal sanctuary.

-Continue to release and notice any thoughts. Wonder if these thoughts are your own. Let them go.

Integrate

Just notice. You are here now. Feel the sensation of this moment in time, inside the center of your own head. Your head feels lighter and your mind chatter is a distant background hum. You've created more space for you to reside.

Sacred Cisterns

Subtle Bodies

Your human journey begins in two places, split between earth and heaven, body and soul. Traveling the seas of life, you first watch your body from the heavens, and as you grow into that body, you begin to see heaven from earth. Standing here, you can open fully to spirit, once more feeling heaven's descent, like a waterfall of light upon you. As it pools at your feet, you begin the ascent through the veils once again.

Where are you on your path? Do you allow yourself to meander, to leap and even to fall, or do you plan for perfection and stick to the plan?

The Mystic's Journey

This *Sacred Gateway* opens onto the middle road, which guides you vertically through the central channel or pillar. Moving from the Lower, into the Middle and then to the Upper realms, you develop relationships with various stages of your evolution. Here in the 3rd wisdom ring in the third level of consciousness, there are five practices.

11
Physical Body
Felt Senses

*Call the earth's energy into the bottom of your feet as you root yourself
into its center, opening the gateway between the material world
and the magical kingdoms of inner Earth
and the lower world beneath.*

How does grounding effect your experience?

Relax your Body, Quiet your Mind

Center

Open your feet chakras to the vitality enhancing energies of Earth and a healthy, long life.

Find a safe place to walk outside barefoot. Take your shoes off and walk around for a bit, feeling the cool grass or the warm sand under your feet.

Now, find a place to sit in a comfortable upright posture with your feet on the floor—inside or outside. Breathe naturally for a bit, until your mind slows and you begin to come into centerline.

Relax: *Earth Energy*

-Squeeze your toes a few times. Lift and lower your heels a few times Lift your toes, pressing the balls of your feet into the floor.

-Now lift one foot, resting your ankle on your thigh. Press your thumb tip into the bottom of your foot—centerline just beneath the ball, massaging gently in a small circle. Repeat on the other foot.

-Return both feet to the ground, relax, breathe and feel your feet opening to the Earth's energy.

-Imagine the energy rising from the core of the planet, into the soles of your feet—through your feet chakras, into your legs.

-Feel the energy rising up through your legs, into your pelvis and then back down through your grounding tube into the center of the planet again.

-Be still and breathe, noticing how you feel as the earth energy circulates through your lower body.

Integrate

Feel your body. Know your felt sense links you to present time, your connection to the deep and subtle energies of the earth. Your feet chakras—the bubbling spring points, open your body to the flow of energy feeding your kidneys from deep in the core of the Earth.

12
Etheric Body

Spiritual Blueprint

The energetic pattern for your body's cellular structure is inextricably woven into the fabric of your blueprint. Breathe compassion and strength into your belly and out into your etheric body. Use this energy to cleanse your cellular blueprint.

Can you sense the difference in your vitality when your blueprint is clear?

Relax your Body, Quiet your Mind

Center

Your etheric body surrounds you, weaving its subtle essence into your skin and through your organs like a blueprint.

Find a comfortable position—sitting or lying on your back. Feel your breath moving through your body, softening your muscles as your bones sink into gravity. Take several cleansing breaths—in through the nose and out through the mouth.

Relax: *Subtle Body Breath*

-Breathe into your chest, filling the space inside your ribcage. Exhale and feel the breath leaving your body, as the ribcage contracts. Repeat this several times, feeling the ribcage expand and contract with each breath cycle.

-Breathe into your chest again, exhaling out into the space around you, filling your etheric body with your heartfelt breath.

-Feel the energetic threads of connection between your lungs, skin and the space around you. Breathe and feel your body.

-Breathe into your lower abdomen, expanding your belly. Exhale to fill your etheric body with your life force.

-Feel the energetic threads of connection between your vital organs, skin and the space around you. Breathe and feel your physical and subtle bodies.

-Breathe into your head, expanding the space in its center. Exhale to fill your etheric body with inspiration.

-Feel the energetic threads of connection between your brain, your face and the space around you. Breathe and feel the energy surrounding you.

Integrate

Feel your body. Know you are capable of self-compassion when you are overwhelmed with thoughts, emotions, and energies. Know your loving breath will fill your body and the subtle essence surrounding you.

13
Astral Body
Imaginal Teleport

*Create the image of a small golden sun beneath your breastbone,
expanding until it fills your whole chest.
Allow it to fill your body, expanding out to fill your aura.
You are filled with heart, breath and incredible power to transport
your soul through the spiritual dimensions of your dream space.*

What kind of adventures do you want to create in your dreams?

Relax your Body, Quiet your Mind

Center

Feel the warm breeze of transformation gently spiraling around you.

Find a place to lie down and rest your body in an open posture. Be sure you have at least 15 minutes to rest. Focus on your breathing for a while as you lie here, settling into the surface underneath you, letting your bones become heavy and your muscles soften like butter on a warm day.

Relax: *Heavenly Cocoon*

-Feel your body as the breath moves through you. Focus on your belly for a bit, feeling the rise and fall, the expansion and the contraction.

-Let your breath gently squeeze the stagnant energy from your body.

-Next, focus on your chest for a bit. Breathe and release stagnant energy from your chest and heart space.

-When your body is relaxed and your mind a bit quieter, feel the divine energies spinning golden threads into a protective mantle that caresses and surrounds your body.

-Feel the warmth, support and protection of this divine embrace as you breathe into the space around your body. Be with this heavenly zephyr inside your cocoon of golden light for some time.

Integrate

Feel your body. Know the integral part of the learning cycle—whether spiritual, physical, or mental-emotional—comes during times of conscious rest. Feel the divine threading through you.

14
Mental Body
Thoughts & Beliefs

*Breathe into your nose, deep into the center of your head.
Exhale down your spine and into the earth's center.
Feel the limitlessness of your higher mind,
soaring into the realm of co-creation.*

Can you expand your inspired mind into your whole being?

Relax your Body, Quiet your Mind

Center

Breathe the connection between head and heart, mind and body through the river in your centerline.

Find a quiet place to sit for a while in an upright position. Your eyes are closed, your feet are on the floor. Breathe naturally for a while, taking some time to feel your connection with your body.

Feel your breath moving in through your nose, into the center of your head. As you exhale, your breath moves down your spine to your pelvic floor. Continue to breathe this way for a while, inhaling through your nose and exhaling down the length of your spine. Notice how you feel in your body.

Relax: *Spinal Breath*

-Now feel your breath moving up the back of your spine as you inhale and down the front of your spine as you exhale.

-Continue breathing this way for a while, deep in your spinal column.

-Notice how your body feels as your breath loops through your pelvic floor and up the spine.

-Notice how your body feels as your breath loops under the curve of your skull, and back down the front of your body again.

-Find your own rhythm as you circulate your breath this way for some time—up the back and down the front of your spine, looping under and over, connecting the two channels in back and front.

Integrate

Just breathe. You are here now. Be with your breath in this way until your internal rhythms slow—the beat of your heart, the length of your exhale, the softening of your thoughts. Breathe until you feel the rhythm of your soul pulsing through you like the blood in your veins.

15
Spiritual Body
Soul Memory

*Open your cosmic gateway, calling down the golden suns of higher
vibration. Feel the energy pouring through you, flooding
your humanity with divinity, awakening cosmos within.
Ride the crest of the spiritual wave to your soul point above.*

When and where are you most available to the energy of spirit?

Relax your Body, Quiet your Mind

Center

Ride the curl, under the eaves of the cosmic gateway.

Seated in a comfortable, upright position, close your eyes and begin to breathe naturally. Feel your feet on the floor, connected to the earth. Your attention is in the center of your head and your root is grounded into the center of the planet.

Relax: *Cosmic Energy*

-Be aware of your breath as it moves through your body, releasing any stagnancy. Feel the earth energy moving through your legs and pelvis, back into the Earth's core through your grounding tube.

-Feel your body's vital energies moving up and down your spine. Sense and breathe as the energies circulate.

-Using your inner vision to see the night sky, find the Polestar (North Star) at the center of the Milky Way Galaxy.

-See the cosmic energy bursting out and raining down from the center of the galaxy, passing through the top of your energy field, into the crown of your head.

-Feel it circulating through your body, down your back, into your pelvis.

-Feel it circulating up the front, fountaining out through the top of your head, into your aura.

-Breathe and experience the energy of the cosmos flowing through you.

Integrate

Watch, from the center of your head, as this river of cosmic energy flows from above, into and through your body, merging with the streams of vital energies already circulating through you. Know the cosmos in your blood and bones.

The Veils of the Three Worlds

There are three veils we journey through and possibly remain within during our embodied lives. They can be experienced as stone walls, trampolines we bounce against, semi-permeable membranes pierced by our intentional arrows of evolution, or a bank of fog. The veils are part of the *Sacred Cisterns* theme in *"Sacred Body Wisdom,"* the first companion book to the *Sacred Body Cards*. In this book, *"Relax your Body, Quiet your Mind,"* they are strategically placed along the practice pathway, indicating key moments in evolutionary time.

Here is a taste of what the veils bring to the journey as you get deeper into the practices. You will learn more as the veils appear in your practice cycle.

Lower World

This is the realm of shadow and rebirth. In nature it is represented by root systems, natural springs and the primordial soup of your origins. It is your feet, legs, mitochondria, the marrow in your bones, and unconscious mind. Breaking through the veil of the Lower World opens the *Sacred Gateway* to the *Elements*.

Relax your Body, Quiet your Mind

Middle World

This is the realm of humans and nature spirits—the elementals. In nature it is represented by tree trunks, their age rings and the nourishment received. It is the trunk of your body, your torso, spinal column, intellect, and human emotions. Breaking through the veil of the Middle World opens the *Sacred Gateway* of *Soul to Soul*.

Upper World

This is the angelic realm of Star beings and co-creation. In nature it is represented by tree branches, Polaris and the Big Dipper. It is your arms and hands, head and your divine mind. Breaking through the veil of the Upper World opens the *Sacred Gateway* into *Gateways to the Heights*.

Rivers & Streams

Esoteric Anatomy

Acquaint your energy intelligence with the rivers and streams inside your body: the many subtle energy channels. Like veins, arteries and nerves in your physical body, these subtle channels source, move, contain, and pool the effervescent essences that nourish you on the mystical journey of life. Fortify their constitution with awareness, sensation, and ultimately expanded consciousness, by following the spiraling, watercourse way.

How does being in communication with the divine manifest in your physical body?

Relax your Body, Quiet your Mind

The Mystic's Journey

As the *Sacred Gateway* of *Rivers & Streams* opens, you begin to acknowledge energy—something beyond blood and bone, a greater level of divinity in your body. You learn, or begin to know, that it is not only in and around you—it is you. Over the next 8 *Stepping Stones* you open to the possibility of communication flowing through subtle channels, in this 4th ring of wisdom at the 4th level of consciousness.

16
Vital Vessels

Circulatory Systems

Stand with your feet comfortably apart, bend your knees, gently bouncing your body while you hum! Feel the vitality coursing through your veins and electrical circuitry.

Can you feel your blood and lymph pulsing through their vessels?

Relax your Body, Quiet your Mind

Center

Hum like a bee following its inner senses to find the nectar of the flowers in bloom.

Find a quiet place to rest, sitting upright or lying comfortably on your back, using props to support your body in any way you like. Close your eyes and begin to breathe naturally for several cycles. Allow your body to feel the weight of gravity and its contact with the surface underneath you.

Take a few cleansing breaths, inhaling through your nose, exhaling out through your mouth. When you are ready, close your mouth and begin to breathe more softly through your nose, deep inside your throat, into your chest.

Relax: *Humming Breath*

-When you feel centered, begin to hum with your mouth closed as you exhale.

-Hum in monotone with each exhalation. Feel your body.

-Hum for the full length of your exhalation, inhaling and repeating the humming as you exhale.

-Practice the humming breath cycles at least 9 times and up to 21 times—inhaling through your nose and exhaling while humming.

-Hum as you alight on the rose of self-compassion deep in your heart center.

Integrate

Center yourself and breathe, noticing how your body feels. Rest comfortably, feeling your breath running through the vital vessels, deep in the rivers and streams of your body. Hum your way to self-affinity. Your vitality is linked to self-affinity and your immunity.

17
Sources

Earth & Cosmic Energy Channels

Feel the earth energy flowing upward into the lower body, cosmic energy flowing downward through your spinal column to meet Earth in your abdominal cauldron. When you breathe in from above and below, you can feel the flood of the divine, even in the densest of places.

How do you navigate your inner rivers?

Relax your Body, Quiet your Mind

Center

May the source be with you always.

Lie on your back in a comfortable position with your knees bent and feet on the floor. Bring your attention into the center of your head.

Breathe in through your nose and fill your body with the warmth of your prana. Exhale out your mouth to release stagnant energies. Be with this for some time, feeling more space in your body.

Relax: *The Lower Cauldron*

-Begin to breathe into your lower belly, allowing your navel to rise as you inhale, and fall as you exhale, releasing any stagnant or foreign energies from your belly.

-As you fill the space in your belly with fresh air, you begin to effortlessly digest the energies of your daily life: food, emotion, thoughts and attitudes. Exhale with the intention of releasing stagnant energy.

-Feel your breath digesting what it needs for nourishment, filling your body with vitality and releasing the chaff.

-Continue to breathe into your belly for a while, replenishing and purifying your vitality, digesting and alchemizing the energies in your lower cauldron.

Integrate

Center yourself and breathe, noticing how your body feels. Rest comfortably, feeling your creative energies expand, deep in the source of your body's vitality. Feel the source of your presence.

18
Anchorage
Chakra Plexi

Surrender to the flow of energy moving in and out. Create sacred sanctuary everywhere. Draw gold lines of connection from the floor of your home, bedroom or reading room, studio, office and any other personal place, into Earth's center.

Does grounding the space around you help you feel more anchored in your body?

Relax your Body, Quiet your Mind

Center

Take ownership of your body and the spaces around you.

Sit upright in a comfortable posture, feet on the floor. Close your eyes and breathe for a bit to settle into a quiet, relaxed place. Bring your attention into the center of your head and be still for a while.

Take a moment to feel the bottom of your feet, opening the gateways between Earth and your body. Sit for a while, feeling your body connect to the planet—grounding, running earth energy.

Relax: *Grounding Spaces*

-Feel the space around you. Feel the energy of the room—the ceiling, walls and floor.

-Feel the stability of the floor and how it affects the whole space—your body, your aura, the room and all its definitions.

-Imagine each corner of the floor is connected to one long central conduit into Earth's center.

-Allow any stagnant or imbalanced energy in the room to release through the grounding conduit, down into the center of the Earth.

-Feel the energy of the room—the ceiling, floor and walls.

-Feel the stability of the floor, its energy and grounding influences on your body, your aura.

Integrate

Center yourself and breathe, noticing how your body feels in this newly cleared and grounded space. Rest comfortably, feeling anchored right here, right now. Own the room for yourself and allow space for others to exist here too.

19
The Riverbed

Sun, Moon, Centerline

Sun and Moon energies meander through you, integrating and balancing. Feel the rivers and streams flowing down the back of your spine from your head to your pelvis and back up to your head again. Now reverse the direction, feeling the circulation of energy, awakening and encouraging healing.

Can you sense the currents of the riverbed in your body?

Relax your Body, Quiet your Mind

Center

The Sun and the Moon dance with one another inside your body, supporting and sustaining the active and receptive balance of life with their primal rhythm.

Sit comfortably in a chair with your feet on the floor, your posture is open and relaxed. Feel your breath moving through your body as you come into center. Breathe for a while, becoming aware of golden energy moving between head and tail with the ebb and flow of your breath. Breathe and feel.

Relax: *Yin-Yang*

-Imagine two streams running alongside the main river—your central channel. They gently meander around each of the 7 body chakras.

-Breathe consciously, inhaling from your root, weaving your breath through these side channels (streams), into your brain. Exhale back down again through the central channel.

-Golden energy flows from tail to head through the side channels, circulates inside your brain, and flows back down through the main river again.

- Each of the side channels carries masculine or feminine energy, together balancing and creating the sacred marriage of yin and yang.

-Be aware of your breath as it circulates up into your head, and downward into your chest and belly. Repeat this breath cycle several times, inhaling up through the side channels, exhaling down through the main river of your central channel.

Integrate

Center yourself and breathe, noticing how your body feels. Rest comfortably, feeling the riverbed deepening, opening, creating space for the divine energies of masculine and feminine energy—the yin and yang inside your body.

20
Tributaries

Lesser Nadis

Imagine thousands of tiny rivulets moving energy through your body—life forces, the whispers of your soul. Inhale up from your feet, into your head. Exhale down again, sending a gentle wave of energy through every cell of your body—a river, nourishing your consciousness and eliminating unconscious, stagnant energies.

Can you feel your breath circulating through your cells?

Relax your Body, Quiet your Mind

Center

Feel the corporeal reflections of your soul forces fluidly inspiring your body's wisdom.

Find a comfortable place to lie down on your back, supporting your body's posture. Notice your breath as it moves into the center of your head and out again through your nose, like a gentle wave rolling onto shore and then back to the sea.

Feel the breath flowing into your chest and belly in the same way. Be with each of these waves for a while, feeling your body expand and contract as the breath ebbs and flows.

Be with your breath for some time as it ebbs and flows through these places.

Relax: *Ebb and Flow*

-Now imagine the wave flows through you from behind—through your spine behind your navel, into your belly. Feel the ebb and flow of breath as it moves through your spine, in and out of your belly.

-Feel the wave of breath flowing into your chest through your spine behind your upper breast bone. Feel the ebb and flow of breath as it moves through your spine, into your chest and out again.

-Feel the wave of breath moving through your crown, into the center of your head, filling your inner kingdom. Awakening you in your sanctuary, the wave rolls through the divine gateway, into your head and out again.

Integrate

Center yourself and breathe, noticing how your body feels. Feel the wave of energy moving through your body. Become aware of your ability to sense spirit moving through you by focusing on the waves of your breath.

21
Streams

Meridians & Fields of Energy

Create unique connections, with the streams of energy deep inside. Breathe into centerline. Exhale, creating little streams through your body with your breath, awakening feeling everywhere inside you. Inhale back through those streams into the main river again.

Can you feel the rugged terrain of inner rocks and boulders as your breath moves through your body?

Relax your Body, Quiet your Mind

Center

All riverbeds have a system of streams that link to nearby waterways. As your breath fills the river between head and tail, your seven energy centers become plump with its nourishment.

Find a quiet place to sit in an upright, supported posture with your eyes closed and your feet on the floor. Begin by breathing through your nose, circulating into the center of your head, then exhaling down, allowing the breath to carve a channel between the center of your head and the center of the Earth through your centerline.

Ground your root into the center of the planet. Focus on your breath for a while, feeling the stagnant energies clearing away as they flow into Earth's center.

Relax: *The Central Channel*

-Feel your chakra centers opening, expanding and spinning as your breath descends.

-Sense each of the seven primary body chakras: the crown of your head, your inner eye, throat, heart, solar plexus and sacral centers; feel the root at your tailbone and pelvic floor.

-Feel each chakra individually as your breath flows, filling each on the way down.

-Inhale to circulate your breath in and around each chakra. Exhale, feeling the breath flowing out into the many streams off the main river in centerline—into your arms and legs, your fingers and toes, your organs and skin.

Integrate

Center yourself and breathe, noticing how your body feels. Be here for sometime breathing—awakening the energy in the streams flowing from the river in your centerline.

22
Wellsprings
Creative Channels

*Feel the spring in your lower cauldron. Its waters fountain up through your body, pooling in the crown of your head.
Feel the energy spilling down through the pools again like water falling over the seven seeds of life.
Your creative energy lights up every cell of your body and every inch of your subtle anatomy.*

Can you feel the energy flowing between your belly, your throat and head?

Center

Feel the commitment of golden energy in motion, a zygote of masculine and feminine, together seeding the flowers of life.

Sit for a while, breathing naturally as you come into center. Ground your root and feel your energy field around you, welcoming earth and cosmos into your body as your breath moves through you. Breathe and dance with the energies for a while.

Relax: *Gender Grounding*

-Place your hands on your lower belly, energetically cradling your gonads—ovaries or testes.

-Be here for a while, drawing your breath into your gonads. Exhale to release any stagnant energies down through your grounding tube.

-Breathe and feel the energy of your gonads.

-Feel the warmth of the sun above you, opening your crown to its brilliance. Feel the reflection of its light in each of your gonads.

-Breathe and feel the sensation under your hands, deep in your body.

-Be with your breath for a some time, noticing the springs of golden energy flowing from your gonads into your root chakra.

-Feel the gentle pulse of these springs pumping a stream of gold downward through your grounding into the center of the Earth.

Integrate

Center yourself and breathe, noticing how your body feels. Feel the sensation of this wellspring feeding the golden river that connects you to the Earth. A fountain of gold pools in each of your chakras, overflowing at the crown, tumbling back down again to the root.

23
Pools of Energy
Cauldron of Creation

The light of the golden flame in your mind's eye speaks the language of your soul, showing you the way in. Massage the top of your head with your fingertips to awaken your crown and the shimmering pool of energy that holds your spiritual essence.

Can you transmute the heaviness in your head with awareness of a place deep inside and beyond thought?

Relax your Body, Quiet your Mind

Center

Bask for a while in the warmth of a great golden sun, breathing and opening your body to its essence.

Sit in an upright posture, close your eyes and place your feet on the floor. Ground yourself, breathing naturally, inhaling to nourish, exhaling to clear and release. Feel yourself arriving in center.

Relax: *The Golden Coin*

-Envision a golden ball of energy hovering above your head, shimmering in through the skylight in your crown.

-Imagine this great golden ball shrinking to the size of a small gold coin.

-Feel the coin drop in through the skylight, hovering in your crown, expanding again into a great golden sphere.

-Feel the coin shrinking and falling gently through the centerline of your body. At each level the coin expands to fill your chakras: throat, heart, solar plexus, sacral, root.

-Spend a few moments feeling the sensations in each location. Notice how the golden energy changes your felt sense and shifts your inner world.

Integrate

Center yourself and breathe, noticing how your body feels. Feel the gold flickering in your skylight, on the ceiling of your sanctuary. The coin contracts to create passage between the chakras before expanding again, filling you with the abundant wisdom of source.

Middle World

Human & Nature Spirits

From both inner and outer perspectives, this realm grows like the trunk of the redwood, into the earth through its roots, and into the heavens through its branches. Only from here can you effect the changes needed for evolution and ascension.

Can you be in the middle world and still experience the energies from above and below?

Relax your Body, Quiet your Mind

Practice: Sit comfortably, engage and release your pelvic floor muscles several times. Feel yourself here and now through your connection to the center of the Earth and the center of the Galaxy. Dive into your inner terrain, for a commune with the memories of your soul. This sets a tone for the coming weeks of practice on your journey and the next veil into the upper world.

The Mystic's Journey

You are human by choice—you came from the heavens to live in this world. Center yourself to look from this moment in time, into the past and the future. Your waypoint is inside you. Go deep into centerline to remember who you are, where you've been, and where you are going from here. Pierce the veil between the mundane and the soulful resources of the inner realms.

Soul to Soul

The Language of Spirit

Learn to speak the subtle language of spirit. Your inherent capacity for soul level communication resides at the seat of your wisdom in various intentions, daily choices and creative expressions. It is intuitive! The Flower of Life, symbolized in sacred Celtic knots and in the rose at the labyrinthine center, calls back your knowingness of the limitless and subtle connections you have to all things.

Do you embrace, honor and cultivate your intuition, gut feelings, perceptions and interpretations?

Relax your Body, Quiet your Mind

The Mystic's Journey
Now the *Sacred Gateway* opens to your subtle, psychic communications and greater awareness. As you grow into the language of the soul, you open your body further to your spiritual inheritance over 13 *Stepping Stones* in the 5th wisdom ring—midway between birth and *Unity* at the 5th level of consciousness.

24
Connection

Grounding

Lie on your back with your knees bent. Inhale and exhale, letting your bones move with the rhythm of your breath. Your body relaxes into gravity, connecting your body to the ground beneath you. Feel the earth's energy tickling your feet and your spine, filling you with life, vitality and presence.

How does your connection to the Earth enhance your relationship to present time?

Relax your Body, Quiet your Mind

Center

Your body is the Earth. Allow gravity to to align and balance your body's structures.

Lie on your back in a comfortable position, preferably on a mat and hard surface. Begin with your knees bent, feet are on the floor, arms resting alongside your body, breathing naturally. Be here, just breathing for a while until you feel a bit more present and centered in your body.

Allow your spine to fall into gravity, no effort needed. Just allow.

Relax: *Imprinting*

-Feel your pelvis and sacrum resting on the floor. Breathe and feel your body.

-Feel your shoulder blades resting on the floor. Breathe and feel your body.

-Feel the back of your head resting on the floor. Breathe and feel your body.

-Feel each of thee bony landmarks—equally weighted on both sides of your body.

-Beginning at the base of your spine become aware of each vertebrae as it gently and effortlessly drops into its proper place.

-Breathe out all tension as the bones imprint on the ground underneath you—some directly onto the floor, others floating in their natural positions. Breathe and feel your body.

Integrate

Feel your body. See your body in your mind's eye. Be here now. Breathe out all tension as the back of your body surrenders to gravity and naturally finds its way—anchoring in all the right places to support its alignment.

25
Origins
Chrysalis

Liquid golden light moves gracefully between head and tail. Sit upright and gently reach your heart forward, arching your back, and then soften your heart as you round backward, creating a wave-like movement. Move with your breath, thoughtful and slowly. Close your eyes, feel your body and know freedom.

Does subtle vibration and gentle movement create a sense of freedom for you?

Center

Your spinal column—its bones, soft tissues, and fluids, is an undulating wave of deep and subtle, constant motion.

Sit upright on the floor in a cross-legged posture; or in a chair with your feet on the ground; your palms rest on your knees or thighs. Straighten your spine as though you are reaching upward through the top of your head to the North Star, and downward through your tailbone into the center of the earth.

Close your eyes, breathe naturally, feeling the connection between your tailbone and head. Find center. Move with your breath, slowly and thoughtfully.

Relax: *The Wave*

-Lean forward and back a few times, moving from your hip joints.

-Circle your torso around in each direction, moving from your hip joints.

-Lean, even bend a little to each side a few times using your hands as support if needed.

-Come back to upright in center.

-Gently reach your heart forward, slightly arching your upper back.

-Soften your chest and round, or curl backward.

-Continue and connect the movements, creating a gentle wave through your spine. Inhale to arch, exhale to curl.

-Gently arch forward and curl backward, slowly undulating your spine.

Integrate

Feel your body. See your body in your mind's eye. Be here now. Your spinal column is a hologram of your subtle anatomy: central channel, chakras and kundalini energy. Move your spine; move your energy.

26
Clear Sight
Clarity

*Nestled deep in your center are the four pillars of your inner kingdom.
Lie on your back opening your chest with each inhalation,
softening as you exhale. Your arms slide and circle around,
gliding in rhythm with your breath.
Feel the energy surrounding you, owning your personal space.
Come inside.*

Have you enough room to hold and honor your wisdom?

Relax your Body, Quiet your Mind

Center

When your inner sanctuary is clear, you can see into the depths of your inner terrain, sensing the beauty that lies in the outer world, beyond the physical form of earthly things.

Lie down in a comfortable, supported posture. Close your eyes breathing naturally until you feel a rhythmic ease in its cycle. Feel the back of your head weighted on the floor, resting and breathing.

Relax: *The Space Behind your Eyes*

-Allow your eyes to drift away from the space in front of you, away from your forehead. Your forehead softens and your awareness falls deep into the center of your head.

-Feel the skin on your face soften as though melting into your ears. Be here, with your breath.

-Be aware of the space behind your eyes, deep in the center of your head—your inner kingdom.

-Feel the openness of this inner sanctuary—the altar of your wisdom.

-Be here for a while, just feeling the space behind your eyes, allowing your awareness to drop deeper with each breath.

Integrate

Feel your body. See it in your mind's eye. Be here now. Feel the space around you. Feel your attention drifting inward with each inhalation, the sounds of the outside world disappearing as you exhale.

27
Expressions

Blueprint

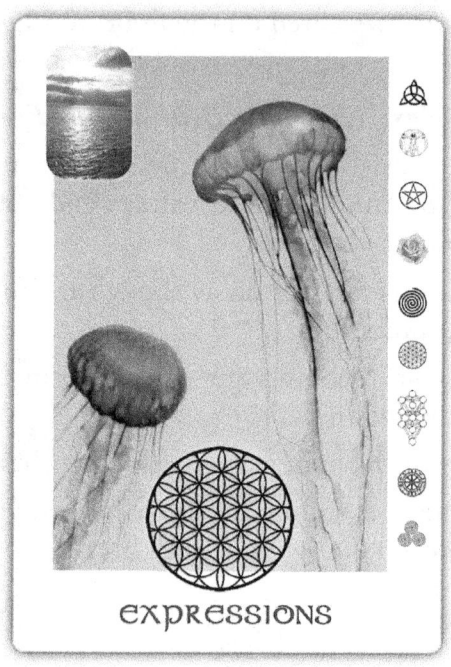

*As you relax your body and quiet your mind, you open the wonder-filled space of connection between body and spirit. As you listen, your essence expresses. Lie on your back with your knees bent, gently rolling your knees side to side in rhythm with your breath.
Let your head roll in the opposite direction.*

How does relaxation play a role in your ability to converse with spirit?

Relax your Body, Quiet your Mind

Center

A rainbow of light arches over you and the full spectrum of ever changing color and energy influences your body and aura.

Sit upright with your feet on the floor, or lying down comfortably, breathing naturally for a while. Breathe into your centerline, connecting with the place you feel most at home in your body.

Relax: *Rainbow Breath*

-Imagine a ball of gold in your heart center. Notice how you feel as the energy fills your chest.

-Feel your breath carrying the golden energy through your body, filling your energy field.

-Imagine a ball of red in your heart center. Notice how you feel as the energy fills your chest.

-Feel your breath carrying the red energy through your body, filling the first layer of your aura.

-Repeat this practice seven more times, feeling your body as your breath directs the flow of each color into its layer of the aura: *orange*—2nd layer; *yellow*—3rd layer; *green*—4th layer; *blue*—5th layer; *purple*—6th layer; *gold*—7th layer; and lastly *your creation of design, colors and patterns*—the outer, cover layer.

-Be with each layer and color for several breaths, filling first the layer closest to your body, and last the layer out at arms reach.

Integrate

Feel your body, see it through your mind's eye. Be here now. Feel the energy of the colors in and surrounding your body. Try this with any color in any layer that feels right to you. Use your intuition—your ability to sense the colors in the moment.

28
Envisioning

Focus

Your ability to envision is limitless. Your ability to create is also limitless. Close your eyes, envisioning a sacred nature symbol—the sea, a bee, a flower or a tree—your choice. Feel the frequency of that symbol filling your body as you hold it in your mind's eye. When it disappears, create it again. And one more time.

Do you set an intention as you drift off to sleep at night, and rise each morning with a vision for your day?

Relax your Body, Quiet your Mind

Center

Imagine a world of inspiration and connection—a moment in time or a lifetime of contentment.

Find time to ground and center yourself, breathing naturally in a comfortable position—seated or lying down. Follow your breath into your body and notice how you feel, experiencing your sensations here for a few breaths. Continue to follow your breath to other places, again, breathing and noticing how you feel. Be with your body and its sensations for some time—as long as you like or until you feel centered.

Relax: *Create a Better Picture*

-Create a picture of the life you want in present time in your mind's eye—your screen.

-Take a few moments each day to breathe, ground and center, feeling that picture filling your inner sanctuary—feeling it inside your body.

-Ground the picture on your screen into the center of the planet, just like you ground your own body.

-Let it release anything that might interfere with <u>your</u> ownership of <u>your</u> creation.

-Feel your body as your picture becomes clearer. Feel your body as you imagine a bubble of golden light around your picture.

-Let it glow, let it glow, let it glow!

-Set your intention—the underlying purpose of this picture and how you will take action.

-Now let your picture go, releasing and watching as it flows into the universal river.

-Revisit your picture each day and give it the gift of golden energy.

Integrate

Feel your body. See it with your mind's eye. Be here now. Fill and surround yourself with the intention of your creation. Take action and wait for the moment your picture manifests in your everyday world.

29
Consciousness

Spiritual Intentions

Your consciousness expands with awareness and experience. You cannot see beyond the door you haven't yet opened. Sit quietly breathing, noticing how your breath moves your pelvic floor. Continue breathing, noticing how your breath moves your diaphragm and your head bones.

Can you embrace the simplicity and effortlessness of conscious breathing? Can you feel how it knocks on the doors of your unconsciousness?

Relax your Body, Quiet your Mind

Center

The cool breezes of autumn and dusk gently sweep away the heat of the noonday summer sun.

Find a comfortable place to sit quietly with your eyes closed. Your feet are on the ground, your spine is aligned. Prop your body in any way that supports your upright posture. Breathe naturally for a bit, feeling the winds of awareness moving in and out of your lungs—expanding and softening your heart and chest.

Notice your body relaxing, your mind quieting. Slowly and intently, calling your attention back to yourself, into your inner sanctuary. Be here for a while, just noticing your sensations.

Relax: *Ocean Fog, Inland Heat*

-Feel your breath moving up the back and down the front—deep in your spinal column between head and tail.

-Breathe naturally and consciously, now feeling the river of breath moving up from your pelvis into your head.

-Feel your breath gently pushing the heat from your head into your pelvic cauldron. Breathe and feel the warmth in your belly.

-Feel your breath gently pushing the fog in your belly up to your head. Breathe and feel your cool head.

-Feel the breath flowing along the rivers in between, gently pushing the fog up and the heat down.

-Continue to breathe this way, just noticing your sensation for a while.

-Feel the circulating energy that carries the natural flow of water and fire inside your body.

Integrate

Feel your body. See it in your mind's eye. Be here now. Notice how your mind calms and your belly digests the circular thoughts of your day. The ocean breeze rides in on the breath, streaming up your back, creating a cooling fog that pushes the hot energy out of your head and down into your belly. The inland heat of your belly presses the fog up again.

30
Impressions

Empathy

From neutral, your perceptions are unaffected by the chemistry of past experience and stressful memories. Squeeze the past out of your organs, creating and embracing life from a higher state of being.
Sit at the edge of a chair, feeling the length of your spine.
Inhale and twist from your waistline, turning to the right.
Exhale back into center. Repeat the other way.

How do your boundaries affect your relationships?

Relax your Body, Quiet your Mind

Center

Like the wind, the ethers and your energy field, your body too is transparent. Allow safe passage for energies to flow through from within and without.

Find a place to sit upright with your feet on the floor. Close your eyes and breathe for a while until you feel a bit less distracted by outside influences. Come into center: your aura, the centerline of your body. Ground yourself into Earth's center, find sanctuary in the center of your head. Sense the energy surrounding you—your auric field is protective and discerning, yet soft, permeable, and transparent.

Relax: *Transparent Body*

-Notice the quality of your aura.

-Feel its lack of resistance. Feel through it to the other side of the room.

-Feel your body gently swaying, like the branches of a willow tree wavering in a soft wind.

-Feel the breeze whispering through your body. Feel the lightness of your being.

-Imagine a bumble bee or a humming bird flying though you, soaring on the breeze. Feel the gentle vibration of its buzzing sound as it passes through.

-Now envision a rose at the front edge of your aura and let it slide right through your body to the back side of your aura.

-Call it thru your body to the front of your aura again.

Integrate

Feel your body. See it with your mind's eye. Be here now. Transparency practice shows you how you manage the every day energies of the world—other's emotions, thoughts, judgements, behaviors.

Like the air, water, and even a flame, your personal energy field moves spontaneously. It can easily take the shape of its container and expands indefinitely and infinitely like ether. Imagine your body is as transparent and permeable as your aura. Breathe and feel your transparency.

31
Balance

Neutrality

*Your inner equilibrium is formed by the interpretations of your
perceptions. Take ownership of the throne in the center of your head.
Envision a golden rose in your hand and
begin to dust and clear your inner kingdom.
Detach from memories long past, finding neutrality
and balance in abundance.*

How does polarity affect your neutrality and ease in your life?

Center

Your inner kingdom is the gateway into the library of your soul's journey. It is the seat of your neutrality, home to your 6th and 7th chakras and eight pillars of wisdom.

Get comfortable, sitting upright with your feet on the floor, breathing naturally. Your eyes are closed, as you come into center. Just breathe and feel. Create a sanctuary inside the center of your head—a space to be still. Each of the eight pillars resonates with a specific frequency: clear sight, inner rhythm, knowingness, connection, energetic and chemical communications, physical body wisdom and sensation.

Relax: *Clearing the Inner Kingdom*

-Feel the pillars supporting the ceilings from the floor of your inner kingdom—between 6th and 7th chakras. Breathe and be still.

-Feel eight golden beams of light connecting you to the center of the galaxy through your pillars of wisdom. Breathe and feel.

-Feel the link between your pituitary gland behind your eyes and the seven stars of the Big Dipper. Feel the connection between your pineal gland deep in the back center of your brain and the North Star. Breathe and notice how you feel.

-Feel the potency of the wisdom in your inner kingdom as golden energy gently swirls around the pillars, clearing the tapestry of preconceptions and beliefs woven from the memories of your past. Eight stars, eight pillars, eight qualities. All golden.

Integrate

Feel your body. See it with your mind's eye. Be here now—still within the quiet of your inner kingdom. Feel the golden energy ignite the wisdom of the pillars—creating beams of golden light connecting you to the center of the Milky Way through your chakras, and glands.

32
Knowingness
Receptivity

If you can empty your mind for only a moment, you will experience the knowledge of the Universe flowing through you. Breathe in to feel your body. Breathe out to release any tension. Breathe in to become more present; breathe out any past-time energy.
Breathe in to fill the center of your head;
breathe out to release anything that is not your own.

Can you allow your thoughts to move aside,
experiencing the moment between breaths?

Relax your Body, Quiet your Mind

Center

Your breath and crown chakra together have the capacity to digest and alchemize all energies.

Take a moment to find a comfortable position—sitting or lying down. Begin to breathe naturally, first into your pelvis, expanding your belly for a bit. Breathe into your chest, expanding your ribcage. Breathe into your brain, expanding your head bones. Breathe for a while into all three places, releasing any stagnant energy through your mouth as you exhale.

Relax: *Alchemizing Breath*

- Breathe into your chest again, then exhale, directing the breath up through your crown—out through the top of your head.
- Feel your body as you direct your breath upward and outward, releasing stagnant energy.
- Breathe this way for about 9 cycles. Sit for some time and feel your body.
- Continue to breathe into your body—anyplace you feel tension or stagnancy, exhaling up through your crown, up through your soul point at the 8th chakra, into the ethers above your aura—about seven feet above you. Your intention is to alchemize the energies, turning negative to useful, dense to light, dross to gold.
- Notice any thoughts or emotions that arise.
- Breathe and breathe some more, continuing to alchemize these energies through your crown and your soul point above.

Integrate

Feel your body. See it from your mind's eye. Be here now. Alchemize and recycle your stagnant and unwanted energies with intention. Shift negative thoughts to proactive thoughts. Reframe your emotions, beliefs and experiences by allowing the breath to carry them through the cosmic gateway at your crown.

33
Telepathy
Transmission

Listen intently for the call of benevolence, to receive and transmit higher frequencies in the world outside. Imagine tossing your negative, circular or overriding thoughts into an imaginal trash can. Watch as the trash can disintegrates.

Do your own thoughts hide your behaviors from you, blocking your ability to receive and interact with the subtle messages from source?

Relax your Body, Quiet your Mind

Center

Be aware of your thoughts—judgements, beliefs and ideas, learning to contain, digest and release them.

Find a comfortable, quiet place to sit with your feet on the floor, or lie on your back. Breathe naturally and easily, noticing your thoughts as they come up. Just breathe and allow. Meditation is never really about not thinking or pushing anything away. Be with your thoughts for a short while as you breathe, calling them up from the cellars of your memory banks.

Relax: *Thought Bubbles*

-Begin to notice the tone of your thoughts, releasing them as you exhale.

-Be aware of how you feel—any emotions and physical sensations as the thoughts arise. Exhale and release.

-Notice how you follow your thoughts into a storyline. Be aware of the storyline. Breathe and release it.

-Breathe with this awareness for 5 minutes or so. Allow the stories to surface—feeling the energy and releasing them.

-Once you've become aware and have taken time to feel the energy of your thoughts and stories, breathe them into a bubble outside of your aura. Send it away and pop the bubble!

-Create a golden sun above your head, feeling the warmth and brilliance of its energy shining down on you.

-Breathe in the nourishing energy surrounding your body, as the golden sun fills the empty spaces in your body and aura.

-Feel the vibrancy of your own enthusiasm coursing through your body.

-Feel the freshness of the golden inspiration that replaces the old stories.

Integrate

Feel your body. See it with your mind's eye. Be here now. Remember, the lower mind follows your thoughts into the drama of past experiences. Your higher mind is inspired, creating anew from higher frequencies. Continue to be aware of your thoughts and how you follow them into a storyline. Know, feel and release.

34
The Witness

God's Eye

*The flame of limitlessness burns eternally within when you walk
through life as a witness. Walk slowly and intentionally
as you hold a sacred picture in your mind's eye.
Know you can call it back if it disappears—
imagination is limitless.*

*Do you empower yourself to observe and change what
you don't like while embracing what you enjoy?*

Relax your Body, Quiet your Mind

Center

There you are, underneath the seven brilliant stars of the Big Dipper, feeling their connection to the seven levels of awareness as they light up the seven endocrine energies in your body.

Be comfortable in an upright posture with your eyes closed. Just breathe for a while, feeling your body. Call your attention into center, connecting yourself to the center of the earth, the center of your head, the centerline of your body. Be in the center of your personal space.

Relax: *The Big Dipper*

-Breathe into your pituitary gland—right behind your eyes. Feel the golden energy swirling and clearing this pillar of knowingness. Be with it until it gleams.

-Imagine the night sky above you—the Big Dipper hovering, ready to pour its enlightenment into your crown.

-Now look for the seven sparks of light inside your pituitary gland. Watch as each of these sparks spins a golden thread that lassoes the seven twinkling stars in the Big Dipper.

-Feel your connection to the Big Dipper—seven energies in your pituitary to its seven stars.

-Breathe and feel the energy of the Dipper dribbling liquid gold down each thread to meet the sparks in your pituitary. Be still for some time, breathing and feeling the connection.

-Breath and receive, and breathe again.

Integrate

Feel your body. See it through your mind's eye. Be here now. Feel the exchange between your pituitary and the Big Dipper. Feel the match. Know your connection to the great constellation at the center of the Milky Way Galaxy.

35
The Record Keeper

Akashic Records

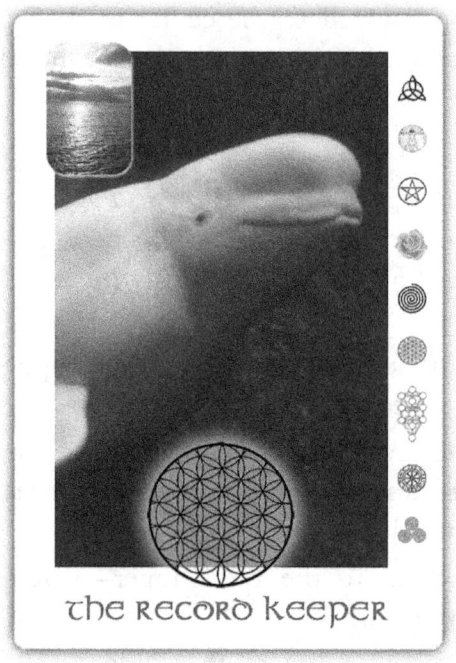

Dive deep into the fathomless sea of unknown spaces, moving beyond time, into the quiet and eternal library at the threshold. Breathe gently, expanding and contracting your chest, lifting and lowering your breastbone. Each time you exhale, repeat the sound, HAAAA, blowing stagnant air out of your mouth.

Do you allow the mental act of knowing to block the experience of your wisdom?

Relax your Body, Quiet your Mind

Center

Polaris lies deep in the center of the Milky Way, the pole around which all the constellations and solar systems revolve. This is true north.

Find a place to lie on your back—under the stars if possible, with your body supported in any way that allows for conscious rest. Follow your breath, allowing it to guide you into the depths of your body. Your inner rhythm is linked to the rhythms of the planet, its moon, the tides and currents, through your pineal gland. Relax and flow, in tune with the rhythm inside, the galactic currents, and the waves gently lapping the shore here on Earth. Let it be.

Relax: *The Polestar*

-Close your eyes and breathe, imaging a golden light spiraling through you, beaming down from Polaris, into your pineal gland. Be with this as long as you like.

-Feel your eyes drift back into the center of your head. Your forehead softens, your breath moves like a slow river deep in your spinal column as your body surrenders to gravity.

-Polaris awakens your cranial rhythms with its divine essence, shining into your pineal gland, down through your centerline, all the way to your tailbone and into the center of the Earth.

-Feel its energy circulating with your breath for some time.

Integrate

Feel your body. See it with your mind's eye. Be here now, feeling the rhythms of the divine flow within. Your cranial tides guide your cerebral spinal fluids. The fluids set the rhythm for effortless breathing, deep rest—clearing away the calcified surface of your pineal gland, uncovering its crystalline clarity and connection to a higher source. Your inner eye is awakened.

36
Healing
Manifesting Change

Show the world your willingness to give, receive and fully embrace life. Clasp your hands and squeeze. Now rub your palms together rapidly, creating heat. Bathe yourself in their warm, transformational healing energies.

How does touch help your connection to
the divine power of healing?

Relax your Body, Quiet your Mind

Center

An expert juggler and an alchemist, you spin your breath into golden balls that melt away, becoming the golden fountain that fills your personal space and makes dreams real.

Sitting in a comfortable upright posture, your hands are in your lap, palms facing up. Center yourself, breathing in through your nose and out through your mouth several times, cleansing your body of stagnant energies.

Relax: *Springs of Gold*

-Breathe in through your nose again, this time exhaling down your arms and out through your palms.

-Be with this breath for some time, continuing to feel the breath flowing out through your palms as you exhale.

-Allow the breath to clear the passage between head and palms, exhaling any stagnant energies.

-Continue to breathe this way for some time, following the path of your breath between the center of your head as you exhale, feeling the energy fountaining out your palms.

-Now allow the breath to pool in the palms of your hands, feeling a ball of golden energy building in your palms as you breathe.

-Feel the ball of gold barely suspended and spinning in the palms of your hands.

-Now the ball turns to liquid as the golden energy fountains out through your palms.

-Breathe and feel the river of gold turn into a fountain of light right there in the palms of your hands, spraying into your aura.

Integrate

Feel your body. See it with your mind's eye. Be here now, feeling the life forces as they fountain out through the palms of your hands, into the world where you greet your life, manifesting your dreams and intentions.

The Mystical Journey

Pathworking

MYSTICAL JOURNEY

Unknown until it appears, the journey unfolds with each step and every breath. The search for truth remains a brilliant and eternal, often wild adventure. It meanders along three very different and evolutionary pathways. The middle road of ease and integration appears to be the clearest and most direct route, yet is often unmarked. On either side of center, the solar and lunar paths simultaneously integrate, reflect and repel one another, yet each leads to a different, less traveled route. Each requires degrees of strength and compassion to bridge the crevasse between them.

Do you struggle to stay on the middle road, or do you take risks to expand and evolve your knowing and spiritual intelligence?

Relax your Body, Quiet your Mind

The Mystic's Journey

Within the *Sacred Gateway* of the *Mystical Journey*, there are three paths and three choices: one is known; the other two are potential new adventures in evolution. It's up to you to decide where you've already been and where to direct your attention while inside the 6th wisdom ring and its 8 *Stepping Stones* at the 6th level of consciousness.

37
Strength
Pillar of Justice

*The door to inner strength opens when you make different choices
nudging you off your normal course. Inhale—engage the
muscles in your lower cauldron. Exhale—release.
Feel the space you've created in your chest
as you breathe deeply into your heart,
readying for the journey ahead.*

Do you react to your reactions?

Relax your Body, Quiet your Mind

Center

Create space for your heart to express the strength of your soul's intention.

Find a comfortable place in a darkened room to lie down. Close your eyes, settle in, and just breathe naturally for a while as you rest. Your experience turns inward, deeper into your heart with each breath. Softening, bone by bone, muscle by muscle.

Relax: *Heart Breath*

-Feel the breath filling your chest, expanding it upward and then allowing the breastbone to sink into your spine as you exhale.

-Feel your breath filling your ribs as you inhale, expanding them to both sides like an accordion. Press the accordion in toward centerline as you exhale.

-Feel your mid-back expanding, pressing gently into the floor as you inhale. Feel your back relax as you exhale.

-Feel your breath filling the whole space inside your ribcage--front, back and sides. Exhale and feel your ribcage moving in towards center from all sides.

-Be here for some time, feeling the space around your heart as you breathe. Feel the expansion and the providence of your heart center.

Integrate

Feel your body. Be here now. Find your way, strong in your center and open in your heart. Find strength in your vulnerability, safety inside your frame. Rest here, noticing your sensations.

38
Compassion
Pillar of Mercy

The steel of the sword forged in fire is more compassionate than sweetness. Your path is a real and true expression of humanity when it is fueled by the strength of self-awareness. As you breathe deeply into your body, envision the constellations lighting up in your cells.

Have you cultivated enough self-affinity to be truly compassionate toward others?

Relax your Body, Quiet your Mind

Center

The stars in the sky twinkle around the top of your head like a halo of light remembering your soul's intention for this earthly journey.

Find a quiet, peaceful place to sit and enjoy the feeling of those memories. Sit upright in a supported posture, breathing naturally for a while. Breathe into your nose, clearing the center of your head. Breathe out and down your spine.

Relax: *Your Halo*

-Look up at the ceiling in the center of your head, through the skylight in your crown into the space just above your head.

-Notice a golden ring of light floating there. Be still and breathe, feeling the light overhead.

-Imagine a golden ball of energy emerging from inside this halo. Its golden light hovers for a while shining down upon you. Then it falls through, filling your body and your aura.

-Be still, breathing naturally, feeling the golden energy of spirit flowing through you. Be here for a while.

Integrate

Feel your body. Be here now. This brilliant gold is birthed from your spiritual essence. It is truly your highest creative potential, co-created from the divine with you. Find your way to self-love, guided by the halo of remembrance.

39
Brilliance

Splendor

Body to spirit communication shines light on your journey inward and opens the door to your next step. Breathe into your spinal column allowing the energy of your breath to pool in the nerve roots at your crown, third eye, throat, solar plexus, sacrum and root. Breathe out through the threads of connection into the chakras in your subtle body blueprint.

Can you be curious about your pain without dramatizing it?

Relax your Body, Quiet your Mind

Center

Follow the energy of the cosmos into your body, awakening the spiritual forces inside.

Sit in an upright, supported and open posture with your feet on the floor. Close your eyes and breathe naturally. Breathe out the energy of your thoughts. Feel your body.

Relax: *Cosmic Essence*

-Breathe into your chest from the top of your head and the bottoms of your feet. Breathe out of your chest, through your arms and hands.

-Feel this breath, noticing the sensation in your body.

-Breathe cosmic blue energy into your chest through the top of your head and the bottoms of your feet. Feel it circulating in your chest. Breathe cosmic blue out through your arms and hands.

-Feel this breath, noticing any sensation in your body as your breath carries the cosmic blue energy fully into your whole body. Exhale out through every pore of your skin.

-Try this with gold or yellow, purple and green, or any other color, noticing how you feel as the energy of the rainbow flows through you.

Integrate

Feel your body. Be here now. Find your way into the pain of your human condition and the subtle yet colorful conversation between your body and spirit. Heal yourself with your brilliance. Awaken.

40
Evolution

Victory

If you fall too far into the well of pride, you will miss finding beauty in the mundane, amusement and enthusiasm for the simple things in life. Cultivate people in your life who will honestly reflect you to you.

Can you feel the difference between amusement and hilarity; excitement and enthusiasm; surrender and succumbing?

Relax your Body, Quiet your Mind

Center

Be aware of three minds: the monkey, the master and the king. Allow the master to quiet the monkey, then listen closely for the king's message.

Now, sit or lie in a comfortable, supported position, breathing naturally. Come into center: the center of your head, centerline of your body, and the center of your aura.

Relax: *Three Minds*

-Feel first, the space on top and just above your head. Call your attention into that place, bringing all of your energy up there.

-Breathe and notice how you feel hovering here.

-Next, feel the space just behind your forehead. Call your attention to that place, bringing all of your energy there.

-Breathe for a while, noticing how you feel sitting here.

-Feel your lower head bone just above the back of your neck. Call your attention into that place and bring all of your energy there.

-Breathe and notice how you feel in residence here.

-Now, take a few relaxing, cleansing breaths and move your attention right into the center of your head, deep behind your eyes, beneath the ceiling at your crown.

Integrate

Feel your body. Be here now. Call yourself back from the pressures of the monkey mind, finding your way into the balance and joy of divine inspiration. Feel its spaciousness in your inner kingdom—the seat of your wisdom.

41
Vitality

Intention

Now is the time to find the seeds of vitality inside your body and utilize that potency to create from the baseline of your soul's intention. Carefully place your arrow, focus, draw your bow, and release. Watch as it flies straight to the target's center. Experience the clarity of your goals when seen through this lens. Kindle the spiritual fire for some time before you lose yourself in ideology.

Are your goals and desires based in spiritual intention?

Relax your Body, Quiet your Mind

Center

Intend to know yourself well. Take time for self-reflection each day—to breathe and be self-aware. Time to let it be.

Sit quietly in stillness for a while—any amount of stillness. Become aware of how you feel both emotionally and physically, what you think about, what you crave, what you are compelled to do. Be here for as long as it takes to be just a little more still and aware.

Relax: *Know Thyself*

-Slow down. Breathe. Feel your body. Breathe again. Be aware.

-Be aware of your sensations, your emotions and thoughts, your attitudes and behaviors throughout the day.

-Be curious about your choices, your actions, who you are versus who you believe you are.

-Wonder if your actualizations match your realizations.

-Bear no judgement—just intention and awareness.

-Slow down. Breathe. Feel your body. Breathe again.

Integrate

Feel your body. Be here now. Find your way through the life force of intention and focus, visioning and dreams. Clarify your mind and body before drifting off to sleep and again upon awakening. Reflect on your day. Prepare your energy for the dream state. Prepare your energy for the next day and upon awakening, enjoy self-awareness.

42
Expansion

Trust

*Be wary of immediate gratification. Expand from a place of rootedness. Begin and end your day with a simple request to experience and awaken your awareness.
Set intentions for your dreams.*

Do you in any way wear the coat of someone else's idea of perfection?

Relax your Body, Quiet your Mind

Center

Your breath deepens into the river of your spinal column, into the safe place within where you know nothing but trust.

Find a quiet, darkened place to lie on your back in a comfortable position. Your eyes are closed and lightly covered. Place a small towel or blanket under your head, and prop up the rest of your body in any way that allows your bones to get heavy and your muscles melt. Lie here breathing through your nose, noticing how your body gently surrenders to gravity.

Relax: *Rest Pose*

-Feel the places where your body touches the floor: back of your head, shoulder blades, upper back, pelvis, legs and heels, your arms and hands.

-Sink deeper into gravity with each breath.

-Allow the front of your body to fall into the back of your body.

-Your chest softens with each breath. Your eyes and face, your abdomen and hip joints, your knees and legs, all softening.

-Rest here for a time breathing through your nose, looking into your heart.

-20 minutes is ideal. Every day is ideal.

Integrate

Feel your body. Be here now. Drift into your body, conscious and relaxed, finding your way inside, quietly trusting yourself from center. Expand from here, true to yourself.

43
Intelligence
Knowledge

Understanding, direction and focus combine in the cauldron of conscious creation. Sit quietly for some time each day in a state of complete quiet and stillness. Be aware of how you feel both emotionally and physically, what you think about, what you crave, what you are compelled to do.

Do you take the time for soulful self-reflection every day?

Center

Physical sensation knocks on the door of emotional awareness.

Sit in an upright position, your eyes are closed, your feet are on the floor. Feel your pelvic floor rooted into the center of the Earth, any stagnant energy slides down the root system as you exhale. Be here with yourself for some time, breathing, feeling your body.

Relax: *Emotional Expression*

-Place your palms on your heart center, feeling your body for a few breaths.

-Feel the emotions that lie underneath the sensations. Be here listening quietly, feeling for a while.

-When you are ready, allow any sadness or grief to slide down the root system.

-Notice any feelings of emptiness or loneliness. Feel these emotions for a few breaths before you release them down the roots as you exhale.

-Place your palms anyplace on your body, listening quietly and feeling your sensation for several breaths. Feel the emotions that lie beneath. Allow any heaviness or pressure to slide down through the root system.

-Notice any anger, frustration or irritability. Feel these emotions for a few rounds of breath before you release them down the roots.

Integrate

Feel your body. Be here now. Find your way by allowing sensation to call out. Wait for the emotions to answer, guiding you through the chemistry of your humanity, ever grateful for your emotions.

44
Wisdom

Experience

The divine is always in search of the many beings and creatures that walk the Earth to share its discoveries through their intentions and actions. Know yourself. Begin to express and share your wisdom with those who can experience it with you.
Be curious about life and others.

Will you take the risk of calling in equal relationships?

Relax your Body, Quiet your Mind

Center

Who you are in a crowded world, with crowded minds and adopted self-images may not be who you are as a soul in this body.

Find a quiet, darkened room. Lie down on your back in a comfortable position, propping your body in any way you like. Create a cocoon with a blanket or sleeping bag, an eye pillow and a lightweight scarf or breathable fabric to cover your face.

It might take a moment to adjust to the new level of containment so feel free to cover yourself in stages, first your torso and legs, tucking the blanket in along your sides. Rest here with your arms and head outside for several moments before covering the rest. Cover only to the degree you remain comfortable.

Relax: *The Chrysalis*

-Feel your body. Be aware of your breath. Change nothing. Just be aware. Breathe naturally. Acknowledge and allow.

-Now place the cover over your eyes, and bring your arms inside the blanket. Rest here for a few breaths, noticing your body's rhythms: your heartbeat, the cycling of your breath.

-Notice the ease and depth of your breath. Rest inside your cocoon for 20 minutes or longer. When it's time to emerge, come out slowly, bit by bit. Wiggle your fingers and toes, uncovering slowly. Lie here for some time before you sit up. Sit up with soft eyes and heavy lids.

Integrate

Feel your body. Be here now. Find your way on the experiential path of wisdom. Be true to yourself from within the quiet of your inner world. Know yourself first. Relationships thrive with equilibrium.

Windows to the Soul

Devotional Practices

*Sincere attention and practice propel you through multiple and progressive windows of new opportunity, into the realms where you realize, and actualize, all things as spiritual in nature. Your body is glorified, spirit's communication is effortless—speaking through you from the god of your heart as the Wheel of Life turns in rhythm with the cycles of the universe.
Windows to the Soul represents the essential nature of all practices.*

Do you resist practice or see its discipline meeting the evolving nature of your soul path?

Relax your Body, Quiet your Mind

The Mystic's Journey
Many journeyers stop just before this gateway, going no further. Do not allow resistance, complacency and unconsciousness to stop you under the glass ceiling. The true *Sacred Gateway* is open only to those willing to embody the knowledge, entraining the body's evolution through dedication and sincere practice. The 7th wisdom ring and its 8 *Stepping Stones* hold the intention for breakthrough as you engage in each of the 52 practices during the year. They are the various platforms of learning for each type of practice. Although they are not part of the weekly practice cycle, looking into the windows will help you take a step beyond knowledge where your knowing turns to wisdom.

Breath of Life

Gateway of Presence

Awakening: At birth or any beginning, you take your first breaths, anchoring spirit inside your body. As inspiration becomes you, stagnancy departs and vitality enters.

What are the similarities between the energies of breath, spring time, and new beginnings?

Relax your Body, Quiet your Mind

Practice: Breathe consciously. The air moves through your nostrils, into your inner kingdom in the center of your head. Exhale any dross or unconsciousness. Do this each night before sleep and in the morning upon awakening.

The Mystic's Journey

Your first breath roots you to your body. Your soul's ownership becomes certain.

Visualization

Cauldron of Creativity

Creation: Every passing moment, every breath you take, is another opportunity to let go of the old and create something new.

Are you able to have what you create?

Relax your Body, Quiet your Mind

Practice: Visualize your next step and make a vision board. Focus on this board once daily for 21 days.

The Mystic's Journey
The pictures you create speak directly to your subconscious mind. No translation is needed.

Running Energy

Gateway of Vitality

Transformation: Calling in the energies of Earth & Sky, you allow the great Mother and Father to awaken your body to its spiritual and soul forces.

Are you willing to feel uncomfortable, experiencing the hurdles and deep resistance to your own stagnancy to transform your cells for overall health and wellbeing?

Relax your Body, Quiet your Mind

Practice: Run cosmic, earth, and your own creative energy through your body, into your auric field. Do this to clear and define your personal space.

The Mystic's Journey

The energy moving through you is sourced from the Earth's core, the center of the Galaxy and from within your innermost vital sources.

Inner Rhythms

Cauldron of Affinity

Synchronicity: Galactic cycles create currents in the solar system; lunar cycles create planetary tides. Earth's tides and currents create the inner rhythms of your being and your relationship to your life as a spirit embodied.

Are you willing to move slowly, thoughtfully, quietly and consciously? Are you wiling to do this enough so you can feel your inner rhythms?

Relax your Body, Quiet your Mind

Practice: Move with awareness, opening your joints and your primary energy centers. Do this to open the gateways so energy flows effortlessly through you.

The Mystic's Journey
The rhythm of your body, breath and blood moves with the tides, the spin of the planet and the revolution of the moon around the earth. Your inner rhythms match the subtle forces of spirit.

Cultivating Creativity

Gateway of Expression

CULTIVATING CREATIVITY

*Devotion: Inspiration comes from within. There are three distinct sources of creativity in your seven primary body chakras—procreativity, co-creativity and manifest creations.
Express yourself!*

*How do you experience inspiration?
How does it a-muse your creativity?*

Relax your Body, Quiet your Mind

Practice: Become aware of your ability to birth new ways of being through co-creation and expression. Do this to express and manifest divinity in your body. Sing and dance your birth!

The Mystic's Journey
Creative energy abounds from above and below, circulating though your physical and subtle forms. They meet in your throat, expressing into the world through your hands.

Self Inquiry & Reflection
Cauldron of Wisdom

Recapitulation: Your willingness to inquire within and self-reflect with honesty and sincerity is the first step in self-mastery. Your desire to simply reflect, rather than project, is the next step.

Can you discern the difference between a reflection and a projection, whether it is yours going outward or someone else's coming toward you?

Relax your Body, Quiet your Mind

Practice: Spend time each evening reflecting on your day, making inquiries into your habits and fears. Do this to make room for your brilliance.

The Mystic's Journey
You create the space to go within and reflect on your inner terrain.

Awakening Awareness
Gateway of the Cosmos

Restoration: Self-awareness is human; awareness of awareness is divine. Call out the unconscious, bringing it into consciousness. Destroy what doesn't work and create awareness of your unconscious gifts.

How much space do you give yourself? Can you be alone in an environment without outer world distractions? Can you go within to the expanse of your inner world?

Relax your Body, Quiet your Mind

Practice: Find a quiet, darkened space to gradually soften your senses. Lie down or sit in a comfortable chair. Close your eyes and go within. How much space can you give yourself inside this stillness?

The Mystic's Journey
You create the space to expand the awareness of your awareness. This is the witness space.

Self-Healing & Mastery
Cauldron of the Higher Self

Responsibility: Mastery emerges when you empower yourself to heal and make changes in your body-spirit framework. Healing the body is one thing; healing the blueprint is another.

Imagine you are the only person on earth—the creator of all. Can you meet and match that sovereignty in your current life among so many others?

Practice: Immediately exhale to shift your energy each time you begin to blame a person, place, or situation for your circumstances. Instead, go within and plant the seeds of responsibility, watching the flowers grow.

The Mystic's Journey
Responsibility for your personal space ultimately becomes autonomy and sovereignty.

Upper World

Angelic Realm

Your branches reach high into the cosmos and the upper realms.
They are only as certain as your roots are strong and anchored,
and your trunk is both flexible and solid.

What helps you to access and envision the energies of the spirit world
descending into your body and its energy field?
What inhibits this ability?

Relax your Body, Quiet your Mind

Practice: Absorb the blue of the sky, the light of the stars and the gold of the sun, filling yourself with the jewels of the heavens. Now exhale and release your stagnancy, to call in the higher frequencies of source and meet your guide to ascension. This will set the tone for the next phase of your journey as you move through the practices in *Gateways to the Heights* to *Unity*.

The Mystic's Journey

Your journey has brought you to the last gateway before reuniting with source and the end at the beginning. Open your body to spirit—the guidance of the ascended masters and angelic realm. This is were you directly link at the threshold to your next step.

Gateways to the Heights

Spiritual Energy

Three distinctive portals open the "way-in" on your passage across the sea of consciousness. These entry points mark and hold the subtle fluid contents that crest and curl on your inner riverbeds. You readily surf the first two spirals of body and mind, yet the third wave of spirit will only carry you through this gateway once you've become a witness.

How present are you in any given moment—are you connected to both earth and cosmos? Are you aware of the subtle energies moving through you?

Relax your Body, Quiet your Mind

The Mystic's Journey

The *Sacred Gateway* now opens through *Gateways to the Heights*. Not only awareness and practice, but awareness of awareness—becoming conscious of your unconscious capabilities, is the key to finding your way back home to *Unity* through the 8th ring of wisdom. Your consciousness is now becoming united with your spiritual energies. Your physical body begins to exist in a lighter form, your experiential consciousness has met and matched your spiritual awareness, and over the next 8 *Stepping Stones*, you focus on your ability to fully embrace the divine descending energies.

45
Body Currents

Nourishment

Blood, lymph, air, hormones and biochemicals are holograms of your etheric body energies—also known as prana or chi. You can find these energetic symbols throughout your body. Look down to see your inner compass imprinted on your pelvic floor.

Can you see the nerve and blood routes circulating through your body with your mind's eye?

Relax your Body, Quiet your Mind

Center

The felt sense of your physiological currents is a symbol of the wheel of life—a compass that guides you through the forest of energy, igniting your vitality along the path of your life.

Sit quietly and breathe naturally. Gently call your attention back from the outside world, into the center of your head. Ground from your root into the center of the planet. Be here for a while, feeling yourself in center.

Relax: *Inner Compass*

-Look down at your root to see your inner compass imprinted on your pelvic floor: pubic bone in the east, tailbone in the west, sitting bones at north and south.

-Sit and breathe for a while, feeling your pelvic bones in contact with the seat underneath you. Rock gently forward and back, then shift your weight side to side, enlivening your sense of the directions.

-Feel the river of water running up your back in the west and the fire in your belly in the east.

-Feel the earth in your bones and the air in your lungs.

-Breathe in to lift and open your chest to the east, gently exhaling to soften your chest and open your back to the west. Feel the water and fire moving through your body.

-Breathe in to open your sides to the north and then the south, exhaling back to center. Feel the earth and the air moving through you.

Integrate

Feel your body. Be here now. Open the gateway to see the elements moving through you. Envision the directions and elements imprinted on your inner compass, as the elemental energy flows from your root, out through the spokes of the wheel of life, into all directions.

46
Earth & Cosmic Energies

Macrocosmic

*Earth and cosmos circulate together, defining you deep in the bones of your subtle anatomy. Center yourself. Place roses at the edge of your aura to represent the four directions.
Smell the roses from a new perspective.*

What if every cell in your body is a starry reflection of the cosmos, or the light reflected in a single drop of dew on a rose petal?

Relax your Body, Quiet your Mind

Center

The elements influence your life in both subtle and grand ways. Imagine the wind on your skin, the sun warming your body. Feel the earth under your feet, the moisture in the air.

Go outside, find a place to rest—lie down or sit comfortably. Feel free to stay inside and imagine you are outdoors. Close your eyes and breathe naturally, your attention is in the center of your head.

Relax: *Definitions*

-Smell the breeze—the scent carried by the wind creates sensation in your body, triggers emotions and forms pictures in your mind's eye.

-Allow the scents to carry you deeper into your body and your felt senses. Allow the scents to paint a grander picture in your imagination.

-Feel anything. Feel everything.

-Now, imagine a rose in full bloom sitting at the front edge of your aura. Keep the rose in view, allowing the picture to ignite your sense of smell, drifting deeper into the sensations it creates.

-Allow the picture to trigger your emotions and your felt senses. Be still for a while longer, just noticing, quietly keeping the rose in view, breathing in its scent.

Integrate

Feel your body. Be here now. Open the gateway to see the energy moving through you, feeling the pictures carried in on the elements: the wind, the sea, the rain, and the dank and earthy humus.

47
Vortexes

Anchoring Energies

*Linking your physical body to your subtle bodies and auric field,
you take ownership of your personal space, and your
certainty commands greater presence in daily life.
Look down at your spine behind your navel,
between and just below your kidneys.
See the golden sun, expanding through the full depth of your body.*

Can you see the overlay of your subtle body onto your physical body?

Relax your Body, Quiet your Mind

Center

Energy waxes and energy wanes in cycles: every minute, each day, and through the seasons. Spinning vortexes lie deep in your spine filled with life and vitality, circulating and clearing, always and forever.

Find a comfortable, quiet place to lie down or sit upright in a supported, open posture. Breathe naturally for a while until your body settles. Breathe consciously into your nose and down your spine, allowing your breath to carve the pathway.

Relax: *Your Vitality Port*

-Feel your belly fill. Be here for a while—maybe a few minutes, just breathing, relaxing and feeling your breath move into your belly.

-Now imagine your breath enters your body through a port on your spine behind your belly button.

-Fill the pool in your belly as you inhale, draining the pool as you exhale. Be with this rhythm and breathe for a time—in through the port, filling your belly; exhaling out through the port again.

-Now imagine there are two streams flowing from the port into the back of your pelvis. From here the energy streams down the back of your legs into the center of the earth.

-Breathe and feel the energy flowing in through the port on your spine behind your belly button—simultaneously moving into your belly, and down the back of your legs into the center of the earth. Inhale to fill, exhale to release.

-Be with this for a while, breathing and imagining. Feel the port on your spine clearing as stagnant energy releases with your breath.

Integrate

Feel your body. Be here now. Open the gateway to see the energy moving through you as you voyage deep in the rivers of your subtle body. Like the moon—sometimes bright and sometimes dark, it flows in concert with your thoughts and emotions, the earth and the sky.

48
Primordial Power
Kundalini-Chi

*Journeying deep into the wells of your center and your roots,
you feel the river of power rising within your core,
up to the cosmic gateway at the crown of your head.
Feel the golden light moving up and down your spine,
pooling in the upper cauldron in your head and
the lower cauldron in your pelvis.*

Can you see the hologram of kundalini in your spinal fluid?

Relax your Body, Quiet your Mind

Center

Naturally nourishing, your cerebral spinal fluid moves with your breath inside its aquifer, without agenda. It is but a reflection of your subtle energies: prana, kundalini, chi.

Sit or lie down quietly with your eyes closed, breathing naturally. Feel your breath moving through your body. Notice where your body receives the breath and where it resists. No judgments, no forced changes.

Relax: *Cranial Sacral Breath*

-Focus on the centerline of your body, breathing up to your head, exhaling down to the pelvis, allowing the breath to move through your central channel and spinal column.

-Be with this for a while, noticing how you feel.

-Allow your breath to pool in the pelvis at the end of your exhalation. Breathing up through centerline, allow your breath to pool in your head at the end of your inhalation.

-Breathe this way for a few rounds, allowing your breath to pool in the pelvis and head before it returns to the river in centerline.

-Now, gently squeeze and lift your pelvic floor muscles (PFM) to move the breath up, and release the pelvic floor muscles to call the breath down. Be with this for a while.

-Soft and steady, engage your pelvic floor muscles with the breath, moving your energy up the spine and down again.

Integrate

Feel your body. Be here now. Open the gateway to see the energy moving through you, from head to tail, the river of gold pooling and nourishing you on every level—its subtle encouragement influencing your physiology.

49
Life Forces
Pulse of Nature

*Subtle, vital energies move through unseen channels inside your body.
Envision the glacier moving mountains, slowly creating
valleys, lakes and streams.
Now use your breath to move the mountains within.*

*Do you see how subtle life forces pulse through your body,
scrubbing out stagnancy, filling your cells with vitality?*

Relax your Body, Quiet your Mind

Center

Your breath nourishes with inspiration and cleanses with expiration.

Take some time to focus on your breath while lying on your back and resting your legs on a chair. Or, you can lie down in any comfortable, supported position. Feel your breath in your body.

Relax: *Scouring Breath*

-Bring your attention into your chest and breathe here for a while.

-Feel the ribcage expanding and contracting with each breath cycle. Feel the front, back and sides of your ribcage as you breathe in and out.

-Direct your breath more precisely now—underneath your breastbone.

-Tap the breastbone with your fingertips to draw attention to this place. Let the breath touch your breastbone, from the inside, deep inside your body.

-Continue breathing in and out, feeling your breath scrubbing the inner face of your breastbone.

-Feel it moving from the base of your throat, along the length of your breastbone, to its very tip. Just be with yourself, noticing what you feel as your breath moves underneath your breastbone.

Integrate

Feel your body. Be here now. Open the gateway to see the energy moving through you, using your breath to scrub your inner terrain. There is nothing to change or fix, just notice the sensations as they arise.

50
Divine Matrix

Human Torus

Feel the river of energy inside you—always in motion, reaching and connecting, blending and merging, fountaining up from your pelvic cauldron, through the centerline of your body, into your crown chakra, containing down into your aura.

Can you see your energy field emanating out from your physical body, connecting with surrounding energies?

Relax your Body, Quiet your Mind

Center

Experience yourself in the center of the eternally flowing energy that is yours, yet not yours alone—the soul and spiritual forces moving through you and all things great and small.

Sit or lie in a comfortable, supported posture. Breathe naturally for a bit until you feel centered, relaxed and present. Ground your root into the center of the planet, imagining the suns' golden rays beaming down from above, penetrating your aura. Be here for a while, feeling center, experiencing your connection to something greater than you.

Relax: *Your Torus*

-Feel the river of energy fountain up from your pelvic cauldron, through the centerline of your body.

-It makes its way up through your crown, fountaining down around you, into your aura and through your body.

-Feel the energy sliding underneath your feet, moving up through your legs.

-From here it moves back into your pelvic cauldron, beginning its course up through your centerline once again.

-Breathe naturally as this torus of energy moves up through your centerline, fountaining out through the top of your head, down and all around your body, under your feet, then up your legs into your pelvis before it makes it way up through centerline again.

Integrate

Feel your body. Be here now. Open the gateway to see the energy moving through you—a force of natural law. This life force is a combination of your personal vitality and your spiritual essence. It flows upward and downward, simultaneously revolving around you—spinning, weaving and connecting.

51
Creative Energy
Wellsprings

Creativity is sourced from within, and revealed through choice and action. A spring of color fountains up from your pelvis while a beam of light shines down from the cosmos, meeting one another at the fountain in your throat. This marriage of spirit and matter travels your arms and expresses through your hands.

Can you feel your inherent creative energy manifesting through your arms and hands in your everyday actions?

Relax your Body, Quiet your Mind

Center

Creative energy flows through every cell of your body from deep within your subtle anatomy.

Sit comfortably in a chair with your feet on the floor, your hands on your thighs, palms facing up. Your posture is open and relaxed. Just breathe for a while until you feel centered, and settled into a relaxed state.

Relax: *Co-Creativity*

- Feel the vital spring of creative energy stirring in your lower caldron, fountaining up through your centerline, circulating through your seven body chakras.
- Breathe and feel its frequency pooling in your throat, flowing down your arms.
- Vitality pulses in the palms of your hands. Be with this sensation.
- Feel the golden sun of spirit in your upper cauldron, pouring its divinity into all seven body chakras.
- Breathe and feel its frequency pooling in your throat, flowing down your arms.
- Spiritual essence pulses in the palms of your hands. Be with this sensation.
- Feel both energies filling your chakras, one from above, one from below.
- When the two energies meet in your throat, they merge and flow down your arms, fountaining into your aura from the palms of your hands.
- Feel your creative energies coursing through you. Be with this sensation for some time.

Integrate

Feel your body. Be here now. Open the gateway to see the creative energy moving through you from heaven, earth and deep within you—recognizing, choosing, having, and manifesting.

52
Spiritual Essence
Human Divinity

Brilliant droplets of spiritual essence shower down from the heavens, into your crown, opening your body to spirit, imprinting the wisdom reminiscent of your origins. Look up to see a halo of light hovering over you. Watch as a galaxy of stars and suns are birthed from inside the halo.

What if the Christ in you was waiting to be remembered?

Relax your Body, Quiet your Mind

Center

Like the constellations in the sky, the cells in your body are infused with the brilliance of the cosmos.

Find a comfortable position, lying on your back in rest pose. Breathe for a while, riding your breath like a river running deep in your veins, arteries and spinal column. Be with this for some time, imagining you are looking up at the night sky.

Relax: *Inner Constellations*

-Now feel your breath soften any amount—its movement is barely noticeable to an outside observer.

-Stay here for some time feeling its subtle fingers smoothing the inner fabric of your body.

-Feel each inhalation warming your bones, your organs and cells. Feel each exhalation releasing stagnant energy. The more you breathe, the more ease you create.

-More ease—more awareness of the light shining from within.

-Imagine each of the cells in your body lights up like the stars in the sky.

-Receive your breath and remember, becoming more and more aware of the light of the stars that lie within, reflecting the heavens above.

-More awareness—more connection to essence. Be here for some time—breathing, aware of the stars as they sparkle inside every cell in your body.

Integrate

Feel your body. Be here now. Open the gateway to see the energy of the heavens moving through you, remembering and celebrating your divine essence. What if the stars in the sky were actually a reflection of the light in you?

Unity

At the Threshold

Only from center where the garden of autonomy grows, can unity be truly experienced. Like the ardent redwood, whose taproot is long and anchored deep, you have a singular connection into the earth, while the fingers of another system crawl just under the surface to all other redwoods. Its hearty trunk supports branches that reach to the heavens. Hand in hand, you too, exist in community.

What part of you is known, both to yourself and the outside world; what part is unknown?

The Mystic's Journey
Unity is at center—the place from which all journeys begin, and all journeys end. It is the womb that births us in the beginning, and collects us in the end. *Unity* is the place of full integration and in a human evolutionary sense it can symbolize wholeness and completion. In this 9th level of consciousness, you become a fully enlightened witness at the threshold and departure point into the great cosmic expanse.

References

Design & Recording:
Lucid Design Studios
luciddesignstudios.com

Intuitive Training:
Clairvoyant Training
clairvoyanthawaii.com

Readings & Sessions:
Sacred Bodies, Sacred Rhythms
sacredbodypathworking.com/sacred-body-cards.html

Restorative Yoga Training & Teachers:
Judith Hanson Lasater & Lizzie Lasater
restorativeyogateachers.com

Sacred Body Wisdom Blog:
Sacred Body Oracle & Cards
sacredbodywisdom.com

Sacred Body Card Companion Books
"Sacred Body Wisdom: Mystical Conversations Between Body & Spirit"
"Relax Your Body, Quiet Your Mind: 52 Ways to Relieve Stress & Go Within"

"*Sacred Body Pathworking:
The Evolutionary Journey*"
sacredbodyoracleandcards.com

Michele Geyer author's page
amazon.com/author/michele-geyer

Shamanic Practices & Ceremonies
Luisa Kolker, MA LPCC
luisakolker.com

Taoist Practices
Body and Brain
bodynbrain.com

Mantak Chia "Healing Light of the Tao"
amazon.com

Yoga Nidra Training and Providers:
iRest Yoga Meditation
irest.org

Bio

Created as support for managing stress and preparing the body-mind to open the door into the inner terrain, *"Relax your Body, Quiet your Mind," i*s the second book in a series of three companions to the Sacred Body Cards.

Michele Geyer is the creator of the *Sacred Body Oracle & Cards* and the author of *"Sacred Body Wisdom: Mystical Conversations Between Body & Spirit,"* a book of symbolism and reflection related to this 72-card path working deck.

She is a certified Pilates and yoga instructor with a focus on the gentle practices: Restorative, Pranayama and Nidra Yogas; a meditation and intuitive teacher.

Currently living in Washington State, her soul's home is in the magical isles of Scotland, England and Ireland; and the lands beyond the mists: Avalon, Lemuria and Telos.

Relax your Body, Quiet your Mind

Michele's workshops have been offered over the last two decades throughout the US; in Canada and Ireland. Connect with her directly about her online and correspondence courses, and *Sacred Body Oracle Sessions:* sacredbodypathworking.com/contact.html

www.ingramcontent.com/pod-product-compliance
Lightning Source LLC
Chambersburg PA
CBHW070553010526
44118CB00012B/1308